IRISH
COUNTRY RECIPES

COMPILED BY
ANN & SARAH GOMAR

RAVETTE BOOKS

Published by Ravette Books Limited
3 Glenside Estate, Star Road
Partridge Green, Horsham,
West Sussex RH13 8RA
(0403) 710392

Production: Oval Projects Ltd.
Cover design: Jim Wire
Typesetting: Repro-type
Printing & binding: Norhaven A/S

All recipes are given in Imperial and Metric
weights and measures. Where measurements
are given in 'cups', these are American cups,
holding 8 fluid ounces.

The recipes contained in this book are traditional
and many have been compiled from archival sources.
Every effort has been made to ensure that the recipes
are correct.

RECIPES

SOUPS and BEGINNINGS

FISH

POULTRY and GAME

BREADS, BUNS, CAKES and BISCUITS

SUNDRIES

PICKLES and PRESERVES

SAUCES

DRINKS

SWEETS

OLD REMEDY

IRELAND

Ireland, known as the Emerald Isle, is a beautiful land of lush pasture, fertile soil, mountains, rivers and lakes.

The country is renowned for simple, wholesome foods such as milk, butter, cream, fish and meat. Home baked breads and cakes are a speciality. But it is probably the potato brought to Ireland by Sir Walter Raleigh in 1585, that is regarded as the mainstay of the Irish diet.

Pork has always been the principal meat, perhaps because of the plentiful supplies of grain on which to fatten the pigs. Enmiscorthy in County Wexford is famous for its barley-fed bacon and crubeen, or trotters, have long been a delicacy. A ham would be boiled first then covered with sugar, breadcrumbs and cloves, then baked. Lamb was traditionally eaten on Easter Sunday and disheens, or black puddings made with sheep's blood, are a speciality of Co. Clare. Spiced beef was very popular particularly for Sunday dinner, as well as game or even goat. In earlier times kid was used for the famous Irish stew which would have been slowly cooked in the pot ovens on turf fires in the Irish kitchen. In the past chicken was rare and would be only served for a special occasion.

St. Patrick is the patron saint of Ireland and on his feast day, the 17th March, a dish of cabbage and bacon is traditionally eaten. Many feast days and festivals are celebrated throughout Ireland and these have a host of delicious traditional dishes associated with them.

The 31st October, the Eve of All Saints Day also known as Halloween, was one of the chief 'fast' days and has more vegetarian specialities than any other day. These dishes vary from region to region, and they include Boxty, a traditional Irish potato recipe which is made into dishes such as pancakes, dumplings or bread; colcannon, a dish of kale or cabbage with potatoes; potato apple pudding and potato apple cake; barnbrack, a traditional currant bread, and applebrack. But, whatever the dish served on Halloween it should have a wedding ring or coin, wrapped up and hidden inside. It was said that marriage was foreseen for the finder of the ring and wealth for the person who found the coin. As the well known rhymes go:

"Boxty on the griddle   "Did you ever eat, eat and eat afraid
Boxty on the pan   you'd let the ring go past
If you don't eat Boxty   And some old married 'sprissman'
You'll never get your man"   would get it at the last"

The burning of nuts to find a girl's true lover is also a Halloween tradition.

The food and drink associated with Christmas is very traditional. Roast goose or turkey is more recent and a spiced beef would have been served in the distant past. Christmas pudding, which is a richer version of the original plain, boiled, fruit pudding is served with brandy or brandy butter and mince pies; strones, a type of oatcake, are heartshaped for Christmas, and Parleys which are similar to potato cakes are made for Christmas Eve. Hot whiskey punch is the drink served and rich iced and decorated Christmas cakes are popular.

Goose was also served at Michaelmas on the 29th September when the bird is young and very tender. It is said that if you eat goose at Michaelmas you will not want for money all year round.

Festivals and fairs are part of Irelands' history and have strong links with food. Amongst those still celebrated is the international Oyster Festival in Galway, the Walter Raleigh Potato festival in Youghal, Co. Cork, the Crab and Seafood festival at Glencolumbkille, Co. Donegal, the Wexford Strawberry Fair and many harvest festivals in August and September. Often fairs will last up to a week with song, dance and entertainment.

Yellowman is a traditional toffee-like sweet, which was sold in pieces at fairs. Dulce an edible seaweed rich in nutrients, is found on the beaches throughout Ireland and was sold in a dried form at fairs. Dulse is served as a vegetable with cream and butter or added to soups and stews.

Dublin, the capital city, has given its name to many of Ireland's famous dishes such as Dublin coddle, a substantial meal including sausage, bacon and potatoes. It is the home of the famous and thriving Guinness distillery. Arthur Guinness, who was brewing ale and porter, a weaker form of stout, started to make Guinness in 1789 and never looked back. The Irish are known for a liking of the "hardstuff": it was an Irish distillery that was granted the very first licence for distilling whiskey in 1608 and a homebrewed liquor, known as poitin or poteen has been made discreetly in Ireland for centuries.

Dublin is also famous for its colourful street sellers, the most famous being Molly Malone, who is immortalised in the well known song:

> She wheeled her wheelbarrow
> Through streets broad and narrow
> Crying cockles and mussels
> Alive Alive O!

Being so near the coast, Dublin has an excellent selection of fish. The renowned Dublin Bay prawns are exceptionally large and tasty and excellent fried.

Salmon is the king of fish and prolific in Irish rivers and lakes. Even so it has always been prized, especially the famous Boyne River Salmon. These are delicious, lightly poached and served cold with mayonnaise.

Herring was probably the most popular fish in the past. Apart from being abundant it was cheap and easily preserved.

It is also excellent for a number of recipes and still a favourite. The choice of fish enjoyed includes haddock, cod, whiting, skate, perch, pollan, monkfish, trout, mackerel, sole, ling, eels and excellent shellfish such as lobsters, prawns, cockles, periwinkles, mussels and oysters.

Fish is most often simply cooked and served with a sauce, such as sorrel, parsley, onion or gooseberry. The potato is the most popular vegetable to serve with fish. Vegetables grow well in Ireland and often the meat or fish would accompany the vegetables rather than vice versa. Carrots, onions, leeks cabbage, kale, peas and rutabaga, better known as swede, were popular, along with herbs such as parsley, sorrel and garlic, which grows wild in the west.

Oatmeal and wheatmeal are regularly used in home baking although the famous potato cake pastry is a mixture of mashed potatoes and flour. In earlier times most baking was done in the home although farls, quarter sections of a round loaf, were sometimes sold in shops or stalls. Gur cake was a special cake made for the poor with stale or left over ingredients. Bread making and cake making was a daily event. Most popular was soda bread the traditional bread of Ireland made from buttermilk and often cooked on a griddle. Teatime is still a favourite meal in Ireland and not to be missed. Bread, cakes, scones or pancakes are served with plenty of butter, jam, honey, or syrup with hot, strong tea.

For the visitor the beautiful scenery, wealth of history, excellent seaside resorts and beaches, good food and traditional Irish entertainments such as song and dance make it a country well worth a stay. As the Irish say: CEAD MILLE FAILTE — A HUNDRED THOUSAND WELCOMES.

CARROT SOUP

Soup has played an important part in the Irish diet from early times. The earliest soup was made with whatever ingredients were available, such as wild herbs, berries or cereals. During the great potato famine Alexis Sayer, famous chef of the Reform Club in London, came to Ireland to study how to produce the greatest amount of food with maximum nutritious benefit for as little cost as possible. He highly recommended soup for this purpose. He became Head Cook of Ireland and soup kitchens and soup rooms were set up to feed the poor.

1 lb (450 g) carrots
2 medium onions
2 oz (50 g) butter
2 pints (1.15 litres/ 4 cups) white meat stock
A little nutmeg
Salt and pepper
2½ fl oz (4 tablespoons/ ⅓ cup) cream
Chopped parsley for decoration

Peel and chop the carrots and onions.

Melt the butter in a saucepan, and lightly cook the vegetables until just tender, avoiding letting them brown.

Add the stock, nutmeg and seasoning.

Bring to the boil and simmer gently for about one hour.

Rub the soup through a sieve or liquidize in a blender.

Return to the heat.

Swirl in the cream, but do not allow the soup to boil again.

Serve decorated with chopped parsley.

FISH SOUP

For the fish soup:
2 oz (50 g) butter
2 oz (50 g) flour
2 pints (1.15 litres/ 4 cups) fish stock
Chopped parsley

For the fish stock:
A cod's head and any fish trimmings available
1½ pints (900ml/ 3¾ cups) water
2 carrots
1 small onion
2 stalks of celery
A bouquet garni
Salt and pepper

To make the fish stock:

Put the cod's head and fish trimmings in a saucepan with the water.

Bring to the boil, reduce to simmer and skim.

Peel and chop the vegetables.

Add them to the stock, together with the bouquet garni and the seasoning. Continue to cook gently for about 1 hour.

Strain.

To make the soup:

Melt the butter in a saucepan.

Stir in the flour to make a roux, and cook gently for a few minutes.

Gradually stir in the fish stock and milk.

Bring to the boil, stirring continuously until the soup thickens.

Sprinkle with the chopped parsley before serving.

CREAM OF MUSHROOM SOUP

FROM BALLYMAKEIGH HOUSE

Ballymakeigh House in Killeagh, County Cork is a 250 year old farmhouse, set in the peaceful countryside close to Cork and the lovely Youghal Bay. Owners Margaret and Mike Browne offer Irish farmhouse holidays, where guests are treated as friends. Home cooking, using only wholesome and farm fresh ingredients, is a speciality.

1½ oz (40 g) butter
1 onion, finely chopped
2 stalks of celery, finely chopped
12 oz (350 g) mushrooms, finely chopped
1 teaspoon chopped parsley
2 teaspoons of coriander
1 teaspoon curry powder
Salt and pepper
1 oz (25 g) flour
1 pint (600 ml/ 2½ cups) chicken stock
5 fl oz (150 ml/ ⅔ cup) cream
A little whipping cream for garnish
Parsley for garnish

Melt the butter in a saucepan.

Sweat the chopped onions and celery in the saucepan over a low heat until soft.

Add the mushrooms, herbs and seasoning.

Cook until the mushroom moisture evaporates.

Remove from the heat.

Stir in the flour and mix thoroughly.

Add the stock, stirring well to ensure there are no lumps.

Bring the soup slowly to the boil stirring occasionally to prevent sticking.

Add cream and reheat without boiling.

Serve garnished with whipped cream and sprigs of parsley.

POTATO SOUP

This favourite traditional soup combines potatoes and bacon, both popular ingredients in Irish cookery.

Four the soup:
1 lb (450 g) potatoes
2 onions
1 oz (25 g) butter
¾ pint (450 ml/ 2 cups) milk
¾ pint (450 ml/ 2 cups) white stock
Salt and pepper
¼ teaspoon nutmeg (optional)
2½ fl oz (4 tablespoon/ ⅓ cup) single cream

For the garnish:
4 rashers of streaky bacon
A little oil for frying
Chopped parsley

To make the soup:

Peel and slice the potatoes and onions.

Melt the butter in a saucepan.

Add the vegetables and cook them gently without browning for about 5 minutes until soft.

Mix the milk and stock together and pour on to the vegetables.

Stir in the salt, pepper and nutmeg to taste.

Bring to the boil and simmer gently for 1 hour with the lid on the saucepan.

Sieve or liquidize the soup.

To make the garnish:

Heat the fat in a frying pan.

Crisply fry the bacon.

Remove from the pan, and dice into small pieces.

To serve:

Swirl in the cream, reheat but do not allow the soup to boil again.

Serve garnished with the bacon pieces and chopped parsley.

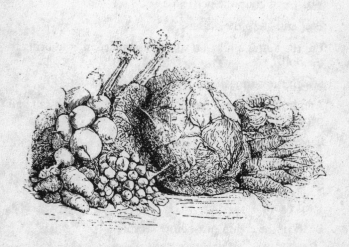

COUNTRY NETTLE SOUP

Nettles have long been used as a vegetable and in home potions to purify the blood and to treat swellings, shingles and measles. In the country chopped nettles were made into tea by pouring boiling water over them, straining and serving with milk and sugar.

Nettle soup was extensively popular; St. Columbia is believed to have lived mainly on nettle soup. Gather young nettle tops by cutting with scissors while wearing gloves. Make sure they are not dusty and have not been sprayed. Nettles are at their best gathered straight from the fields between April and May before they become tough.

1 oz (25 g) butter
1 oz (25 g) flake oatmeal
4 cups of nettle tops
1 onion
1 pint (600 ml/ 2½ cups) milk
½ pint (300 ml/ 1¼ cups) white stock
Salt and pepper
1 teaspoon chopped parsley
¼ pint (150 ml/ ⅔ cup) cream (optional)

Wash and chop the nettle tops.

Peel and chop the onions.

Put the butter, milk and stock in a saucepan, and bring to the boil.

Stir in the oatmeal and return to the boil.

Add the nettles, and season the soup to taste with salt and pepper.

Cover, and simmer for about 45 minutes.

Add the parsley and cook for a further 3 minutes.

Sieve or liquidize the soup if preferred.

Heat again.

Swirl in the cream just before serving.

BROTCHAN ROY - Leek and Oatmeal Broth

In hard times, when meat and fish were scarce, soup was made from vegetables and thickened with oatmeal. This dish was called Brotchan, the old Gaelic word for broth.

3 leeks
1 oz (25 g) butter
3 oz (75 g) flake oatmeal
1 pint (600 ml/ 2½ cups) white stock
½ pint (300 ml/ 1¼ cups) milk
Salt and pepper to taste
A pinch of mace
Chopped parsley
2 tablespoons of single cream

Wash the leeks thoroughly and chop into chunks.

Melt the butter gently in a saucepan not allowing it to brown.

Add the oatmeal and fry it in the butter, stirring until golden brown.

Still stirring, pour on the stock and milk.

Add the chopped leeks, salt, pepper and mace.

Bring to the boil, and then simmer for about 30 minutes until the broth is thick.

Put the soup through a sieve or liquidize in a blender.

Reheat gently.

Stir in the cream and parsley not allowing the soup to boil again before serving with Irish Soda Bread (see recipe).

COCKLE SOUP

Serves 4-6

Cockle soup is famous from the Dundrum area of Country Down. Related to the clam, cockles are found in abundance on many Irish beaches. In Kerry they are known as carpet shells, and in the east they are found among other places in Dublin Bay. They are traditionally dug up as the tide goes out with iron spoons and put into tin cans. Their whereabouts is given away by little mounds in the sand.

About 30 cockles
1 oz (25 g) butter
2 onions
3 celery stalks
1 oz (25 g) cornflour
1 pint (600 ml/ 2½ cups) milk
½ pint (300 ml/ 1¼ cups) cockle stock
Salt and pepper
Chopped parsley
2 tablespoons of whipped cream

Wash and scrub the cockles well, discarding any that are open.

Put into a saucepan and cover with salted water.

Bring to the boil, and cook until the shells are open.

Remove at once or the cockles will toughen.

Shell the cockles.

Strain and reserve the cockle stock.

Peel and chop the onions.

Prepare and chop the celery.

Melt the butter in a saucepan.

Add the vegetables and cook gently until soft.

Mix the cornflour to a thin cream with a little of the milk.

Add the milk, cornflour and ½ pint (300 ml/ 1¼ cups) of the cockle stock.

Bring the to the boil and simmer for 10 minutes or until the vegetables are cooked and the soup has thickened.

Season to taste.

Add the cockles and chopped parsley.

Heat gently for a few minutes.

Serve topped with whipped cream.

LOUGH NEAGH BOUILLABAISSE

FROM THE DUNADRY INN, DUNADRY Serves 8-10

Lough Neagh provides an abundance and variety of sea food such as eels, pollan, trout, perch and grunt (young perch). Pollan, an oily fish, which is only found in this water, is fried or used in soups. The nearby Dunadry Inn serves seasonal produce and specialises in fish dishes like this one, using fish from the Lough.

2 lb (900 g) pike on the bone, descaled
½ lb (225 g) perch on the bone, skinned
½ lb (225 g) eels on the bone, skinned
½ lb (225 g) bream fillets, skinned
½ lb (225 g) pollan (powan or whitefish in Scotland)
**   fillets, skinned**
1 clove garlic, chopped
2 oz (50 g) onion, finely chopped
2 oz (50 g) plain flour
2 medium carrots, chopped
1 stick celery, chopped
2 tablespoons tomato purée
Saffron to taste
Fish stock
1 glass Irish whiskey (double)
1 lb (450 g) potatoes
Butter for cooking

Cut all the fish into 2 inch (5 cm) pieces.

Leave the fish on the bone when stated.

Saute the garlic and onion in a pan with a little butter.

Toss the pieces of fish in the flour and add to the pan.

Cook for a few minutes until the fish is lightly browned.

Remove the fish and add the carrot, celery, tomato purée and saffron.

Stir in the fish stock.

Add the fish and the whiskey.

Bring to the boil and simmer gently for 15-20 minutes.

Peel, slice and lightly fry the potatoes and serve separately.

Dish up the Bouillabaisse in two tureens. One with the fish and a little of the cooking liquid; the other with the soup.

Accompany with croutons, rubbed with a little garlic, and mayonnaise flavoured with a little saffron.

TRADITIONAL IRISH BREAKFAST Serves 4

8 rashers of bacon
4 sausages
4 tomatoes
4 cold cooked pieces of Irish potato bread or
  fadge (see recipe)
4 slices of white pudding
4 eggs

Remove the rinds from the bacon and prick the sausages.

Fry or grill the sausages and bacon until the sausages are brown on all sides and the bacon is cooked to taste.

Keep hot.

Cut the tomatoes in half.

Grill or fry the tomatoes in the bacon fat.

Fry the fadge, white pudding and eggs in the bacon fat.

Serve with soda bread.

CHICKEN LIVER PATÉ

1½ lbs (675 g) chicken livers
3 oz (75 g) butter
1 onion
1 clove of garlic
1 tablespoon double cream
2 fl oz (3 tablespoons/ ¼ cup) tomato paste
2 fl oz (3 tablespoons/ ¼ cup) sherry

Melt the butter in a frying pan.

Fry the chicken livers gently.

Peel and finely chop the onion.

Skin and crush the clove of garlic.

Add the onions and garlic to the pan.

Reduce the heat, cover and cook gently for about 5 minutes.

Remove from the heat.

When the mixture has cooked, add the cream, tomato paste and sherry.

Rub the mixture through a sieve or blend in a liquidizer.

Pack into individual paté dishes, and chill.

DUBLIN BAY PRAWN COCKTAIL   Serves 4

True Dublin Bay Prawns are exceptionally large, with a fine flavour and appearance. In times past women would cook the freshly caught prawns and sell them in the streets of Dublin City. They are most popular today in cocktails or deep fried.

For the prawn cocktails:
24 Dublin Bay prawns
Lettuce
Chopped parsley
¼ pint (150 ml/ ⅔ cup) tomato ketchup
1 dessertspoon vinegar
1 teaspoon piquant sauce, such as Worcester
1 teaspoon horseradish sauce
A pinch of celery salt
A pinch of cayenne pepper
Juice of a lemon
4 tablespoon of cream

Shell the prawns to remove the black 'vein' down the back.

Cut 16 of the prawns up into small pieces.

Shred the lettuce and use to line four cocktail glasses.

Mix the tomato ketchup, vinegar, piquant sauce, horseradish sauce, celery salt, pepper and lemon juice together.

Blend in the cream and prawn meat.

Divide the mixture between the glasses.

Cut the remaining 8 prawns in half lengthwise.

Arrange four halves on top of each cocktail.

Serve chilled and sprinkled with finely chopped parsley.

BAKED SALMON

Serves 4

Abundant in Irish waters, the salmon is often mentioned in legends, writings and poems. It can be poached and eaten with mayonnaise but is also baked, potted, grilled and cured. In the past, the prolific salmon was also pickled.

4 salmon steaks
2 lemons
2 oz (50 g) butter, melted
A little chopped parsley and chives
Salt and pepper
½ pint (300 ml/ 1¼ cups) cream

Squeeze the juice from the lemons and rub into the salmon.

Brush each steak with melted butter.

Season with salt and pepper.

Sprinkle with parsley and chives.

Place in a greased ovenproof dish covered with foil.

Bake in a moderately hot oven for about 20 minutes.

Remove from the oven, pour over the cream and return to the oven for a further 5-10 minutes.

Oven: 375°F/190°C Gas Mark 5 for a total 30-35 minutes.

LING WITH ONION SAUCE

Ling, a large white fish was popular for Friday dinner and other fast days.
It was usually eaten with potatoes. Ling is most often sold in dried form.
The curing was done on the west coast of Ireland where the fish could be
seen hanging up to dry in the shops and even in the hedgerows in the summer
months.

**4 portions dried ling (previously cut into pieces and
soaked overnight)**
Milk
4 potatoes baked in the oven
Onion sauce

Heat the milk.

Add the pieces of ling and bring to the boil.

Simmer for about 30 minutes or until the fish is tender.

Serve with Onion Sauce (see recipe) and jacket potatoes.

MACKEREL WITH GOOSEBERRY SAUCE

Serves 4

Traditionally fresh mackerel is boiled in seawater. When fried it is excellent accompanied by gooseberry, fennel or horseradish sauce, which being sharp to taste cuts the oiliness of the fish

4 mackerel
Salt and pepper
2 oz (50 g) melted butter

For the gooseberry sauce:
½ (225 g) gooseberries, top and tailed
4 oz (100 g) sugar
1 oz (25 g) butter
1 tablespoon chopped fennel

Wash and dry the mackerel.

Season with salt and pepper.

Brush each fish with melted butter on both sides.

Cook in a heavy pan for a few minutes on each side.

Keep warm.

To make the gooseberry sauce:

Place the gooseberries in the pan with the sugar and a little water.

Cook gently until tender.

Stir in the butter, cut into small pieces and add the fennel.

Serve with the fish.

HADDOCK WITH CREAM

Serves 4

2 lbs (900 g) haddock fillet
1 onion
1 clove garlic
A little oil for cooking
Salt and pepper

Peel and chop the onion and garlic.

Heat a little oil in a stew pan and sauté the onion and garlic for a few minutes.

Add the fish on top and continue cooking for 2 minutes over a moderate heat.

Turn the fillets and season to taste.

Add the cream, bring to the boil and remove from the heat.

Cover the pan and bake in a moderate oven for 8-10 minutes.

Serve the fish with the sauce poured over.

Oven: 350°F/180°C Gas Mark 4

WHITING BAKED WITH ONION   Serves 4

FROM THE KING SITRIC RESTAURANT

This famous fish restaurant in Howth overlooks Dublin Bay.

2 lbs (900 g) whiting
Salt and pepper
3 or 4 tomatoes
1 medium onion
A little freshly chopped parsley and other optional herbs
   such as tarragon and chives
2 oz (50 g) breadcrumbs
2 oz (50 g) butter
A glass of wine or fish stock

Wash the fish and place the portions in a buttered ovenproof dish.

Season each fish with salt and pepper.

Peel and dice the tomatoes.

Mix together the chopped onion and herbs.

Spread evenly over each fish.

Sprinkle breadcrumbs on the top and dot with butter.

Pour over the wine or stock and bake in a very moderate oven for about 15-20 minutes.

Place under a hot grill for a few minutes before serving.

Oven: 325°F/160°C Gas Mark 3 for 15-20 minutes.

OATMEAL FRIED HERRING

Serves 2

Herring is a highly nutritous and tasty fish that has been important to the Irish for centuries. Quantities of herring were salted to preserve them and herring was used in many recipes. This simple method of frying herring with oatmeal makes a very good supper. It used to be particularly popular after the harvest.

4 fresh herrings
3 oz (75 g) oatmeal
1 lemon
¼ pint (150 ml/ ⅔ cup) milk
Salt and pepper
Oil or fat for frying

Remove the scales, head and tail of the fish.

Wash and dry the fish thoroughly.

Squeeze the juice of the lemon with the milk.

Mix the oatmeal with the salt and pepper.

Heat the oil or fat in a frying pan.

Dip each herring into the milk and roll in the oatmeal, until well covered.

Fry the fish for a few minutes on each side.

Drain on paper and serve with potatoes.

SOLE AND MUSSELS 'CAPTAINS STYLE'

Serves 4

Another speciality of White's Hotel, Wexford.

1½ lbs (675 g) mussels cooked, bearded and shelled
4 sole, 10-12 oz (275 g - 350 g) each
¼ lb (100g) mushrooms, sliced
½ pint (300 ml/ 1¼ cups) fish velouté (thickened fish stock)
¼ lb (100g) butter
¼ pint (150 ml/ ⅔ cup) fresh cream
½ pint (300 ml/ 1¼ cups) Court Bouillon (make by simmering together water, white wine, onion, lemon, white peppercorns and parsley stalks)

Remove the black skin from the sole.

Run a sharp knife through the back bone of each fish and partly remove the fillets on both sides.

Fold back.

Break the backbone in two or three places.

Lightly poach the fillets in the Court Bouillon.

Sweat the mushrooms in the butter.

Add the velouté and cook for a few minutes.

Add the mussels to the sauce and stir in the cream and a knob of butter.

Gently remove the fish from the sauce.

Discard the centre bone and wing bones of each fish.

Fill the cavity of each fish with the mussel mixture.

The fish can be lightly browned under a hot grill with a little whipped cream spooned on top if desired.

WEXFORD MUSSELS IN RUM SAUCE

FROM WHITE'S HOTEL   Serves 2

White's Hotel is situated in the heart of the busy town of Wexford. White's was originally a coaching Inn, and for centuries has offered fine food and hospitality to travellers including those who arrive at the nearby port of Rosslare. This is the chef's own recipe using local mussels in a rich rum sauce.

1 lb (450 g) shelled and bearded mussels
½ lb (225 g) smoked streaky bacon
1 oz (25 g) onion, chopped
1½ oz (40 g) mushrooms, sliced
1 oz (25 g) pepper, diced
1 oz (25 g) parsley, chopped
½ measure of dark rum
3 oz (75 g) fish velouté (fish stock thickened with
    a little flour)
¼ pint (150 ml/ ⅔ cup) fresh cream
6 oz (175 g) cooked fresh spinach
½ oz (15 g) butter

Wrap 2-3 mussels in each slice of bacon and secure with a cocktail stick.

Melt the butter in a pan.

Sauté the mussels gently in the pan for a few minutes.

Add the onions, mushrooms and peppers and continue cooking for a minute.

Add the rum and flambé.

Remove the mussels from the pan and discard the cocktail sticks.

Place the prepared spinach on a serving dish.

Arrange the mussels on top.

Add the cream and velouté to the onion, peppers and mushrooms in the pan.

Cook over a gentle heat for 2 minutes.

Pour the sauce over the mussels and spinach and serve immediately.

CRAB SUPPER

Serves 4-6

1 lb (450 g) crabmeat
2 oz (50 g) onion, chopped
2 oz (50 g) mushroom, sliced
2 tomatoes, sliced
7 fl oz (200 ml/ ¾ cup) cream
2 teaspoons Worcester sauce
Salt and cayenne pepper
Oil for cooking
2 oz (50 g) grated cheese

Fry the onion in the heated oil until transparent.

Add the mushrooms and tomatoes and continue cooking for a few minutes.

Add the crabmeat and cook for further 5 minutes.

Remove from the heat.

Stir in the cream, Worcester sauce, salt and cayenne pepper.

Pour into an ovenproof dish or individual scallop shells.

Sprinkle the top with grated cheese and bake in a moderately hot oven for 15 minutes.

Oven: 400°F/200°C Gas Mark 6 for 15 minutes.

FRIED OYSTERS

Serves 2

Oysters which are now considered a delicacy were once prolific enough to be the food of the poor. There are extensive oyster beds in Ireland, the most famous are in Galway.

Oysters are frequently eaten raw with a pint of beer or Guinness. They are also delicious lightly fried.

24 oysters
1 egg, beaten
2 fl oz (3 tablespoons/ ¼ cup) milk
1 tablespoon parsley, finely chopped
Salt
Cayenne pepper
8 oz (225 g) breadcrumbs
Fat or oil for cooking

Open the oysters and cook them in a pan of boiling water for a few minutes.

Remove, beard, drain and dry the oysters.

Beat the egg with the milk.

Season with salt and cayenne pepper and add the finely chopped parsley.

Dip each oyster into the egg mixture and then roll in the breadcrumbs.

Heat the fat in a pan.

Fry each oyster for a few minutes on each side, or until golden brown.

Drain on absorbent paper and serve.

GAELIC CHICKEN

Serves 2

FROM THE HOWTH LODGE HOTEL

The Howth Lodge Hotel (former home of a Viceroy) now owned by the Hanratty family, stands in its own grounds overlooking Dublin Bay in the quaint old fishing village of Howth. From the hotel there is a spectacular view of Ireland's Eye and Lambay Islands. Local produce is a speciality - fish, properly hung meat and fresh vegetables. This delicious dish can be varied with the addition of a little nutmeg, or the zest of an orange or lemon.

2 breasts of chicken from a 4 lb (1.75 kg) bird
Oil for frying
½ pint (300 ml/ 1¼ cup) chicken stock
2 tablespoons double cream
2 tablespoon Irish whiskey
Salt and pepper
2 oz (50 g) mushrooms
A little butter if required

Slice the chicken breasts.

Heat the oil in a frying pan.

Fry the chicken until tender but do not allow it to brown.

Remove the chicken from the pan and keep hot.

Thinly slice the mushrooms and blanch in boiling water - or sauté for a few moments in a little butter.

Strain off the surplus oil from the pan.

Add the chicken stock, and season with salt and pepper to taste.

Bring to the boil and simmer until reduced by half.

Add the sliced mushrooms and stir in the cream and Irish whiskey, but do not allow the sauce to boil again.

Pour the sauce over the chicken to serve.

COTTAGE CHICKEN IN THE POT

Serves 4-5

Traditionally this delicious dish would have been cooked in a black three legged pot suspended over a turf fire. A rabbit can be cooked in the pot in the same way.

2 onions or leeks
4 carrots
A sprig of thyme or parsley
A sprig of mace
3 lb (1.5 kg) chicken
Salt and pepper
2 rashers of fat bacon
About ½ pint (300 ml/ 1¼ cups) chicken stock,
  preferably made from the giblets
1 oz (25 g) cornflour
A little milk

Peel and slice the onions or leeks, and carrots.

Arrange the vegetables in the bottom of an ovenproof casserole.

Finely chop the mace and thyme or parsley.

Put the prepared chicken on top of the vegetables and herbs.

Season with salt and pepper.

Remove the rinds from the bacon, and cut it into strips.

Arrange the bacon strips over the chicken.

Pour over the stock.

Cover closely and cook in a moderately hot oven for 1½ hours or until the chicken is tender.

If the gravy reduces too much during the cooking time add a little more stock or hot water.

Strain off the gravy and retain.

Put the chicken and vegetables on a serving dish and keep hot.

Stir in the cornflour into the milk to make a thin cream.

Put the gravy into a saucepan.

Stir in the cornflour, and bring to the boil.

Simmer stirring continuously until the gravy thickens.

Spoon a little gravy over the chicken and put the rest in a sauceboat.

Serve the chicken garnished with chopped parsley.

Oven: 375°F/220°C Gas Mark 5

FARMHOUSE CHICKEN CASSEROLE

Serves 4

4 chicken pieces or 1 chicken weighing about 3 lbs
   (1.5 kg)
2 oz (50 g) butter or oil for frying
4 rashers of bacon
2 onions
2 carrots
2 oz (50 g) flour
Salt and pepper
1 pint (600 ml/ 2½ cups) chicken stock
A pinch of mixed herbs
Chopped parsley

Skin the pieces - or skin and joint the chicken.

Remove the rind and cut the bacon into small pieces.

Peel and slice the onions and carrots.

Heat the fat in a frying pan.

Fry the bacon, onions and carrots for a few minutes.

Remove the vegetables and put them into a casserole.

Roll the chicken pieces in the seasoned flour.

Fry the chicken until golden on both sides.

Remove and put into the casserole.

Add any remaining flour to the fat in the frying pan and
cook to make a roux.

Gradually stir in the stock, and bring to the boil, still stirring,
until the liquid thickens.

Add the mixed herbs, and more seasoning to taste if
required.

Pour into the casserole.

Cover and cook in a moderate oven for about 1 hour.

Sprinkle with the chopped parsley before serving straight from the casserole accompanied by boiled, new or jacket potatoes.

Oven: 350°F/180°C Gas Mark 4

BOILED TURKEY

Serves 6-8

As well as the more usual method of roasting, turkeys can be successfully boiled. Smaller birds are the most suitable for this method, which is centuries old. Serve the bird with the traditional accompaniment - celery sauce - and the usual trimmings, such as small sausages and bacon rolls.

1 prepared turkey weighing about 8 lbs (3.5 kg)
Salt and pepper
2 onions
4 carrots
Bouquet garni

Peel the vegetables, but leave them whole.

Put the turkey and vegetables into a large saucepan.

Cover with cold water.

Season with salt and pepper and add the bouquet garni.

Bring the the boil and skim.

Cover and simmer for 1½ hours or until the bird is tender.

Take the turkey out of the saucepan.

Strain the stock and retain to make the Celery Sauce (see recipe).

Arrange on a serving dish and keep warm.

ROAST GOOSE

Serves 10

In Ireland roast goose is traditionally eaten in Michaelmas Day (the 29th September), as well as at Christmas time or New Year. It used to be accompanied by onion sauce, although today apple sauce is frequently served. The potato stuffing is excellent with goose as it absorbs some of the goose fat.

1 prepared goose weighing 10-12 lbs (4.5 kg - 5.5 kg)
Potato stuffing (see recipe)
Salt
Watercress to garnish

For the gravy:
2 oz (50 g) flour
1½ pints (900ml/ 3¾ cups) stock

To roast the goose:

Stuff the neck cavity of the bird, and secure the flap with a skewer or by sewing.

Put the goose into a baking tin, and sprinkle it with salt.

Cover the bird with tinfoil, and roast in a hot oven for half an hour, then lower the heat to moderate and cook for a further 20 minutes to each pound.

Baste the bird several times during the cooking time and remove the foil for the last 20 minutes to allow the skin to crisp and brown.

Place the goose on a serving dish and keep hot.

To make the gravy:

Strain off the fat, leaving only about 2 tablespoons in the pan.

Stir in the flour and cook to make a roux.

Gradually stir in the stock.

Bring to the boil and simmer stirring continuously until the gravy thickens.

Serve in a sauceboat with the goose garnised with watercress and accompanied by apple sauce.

Oven: 400°F/200°C Gas Mark 6

Reduce to: 350°F/180°C Gas Mark 4

POTATO STUFFING

This stuffing was traditionally used with ducks and geese. Today the mixture is often used to make a potato pie. If using to stuff a bird, the liver may be chopped and fried with the onion.

1 lb (450 g) potatoes
1 onion
1 oz (25 g) butter
Salt and pepper
A little thyme
A little sage

Peel and slice the potatoes.

Put in a saucepan of cold water.

Bring to the boil and simmer until tender.

Drain and mash.

Melt the butter in a frying pan and fry the onion until soft.

Add to the mashed potato.

Stir in the herbs and season the mixture to taste.

Use either as a stuffing for a bird or put the mixture into an ovenproof dish and brown under a hot grill.

CASSEROLE OF PIGEONS

Serves 8

4-6 pigeons, depending on size and appetite
Seasoned flour
Oil for frying
4 oz (100 g) bacon
4 carrots
2 onions
2 oz (50 g) flour
1½ pints (900ml/ 3¾ cups) white stock
1 tablespoon of tomato paste
Salt and pepper
8 oz (225 g) mushrooms

Joint the prepared birds.

Roll the joints in the seasoned flour.

Heat the oil in a frying pan.

Fry the pigeon joints, and put in an ovenproof casserole.

Remove the rinds from the bacon and chop.

Peel and slice the carrots and onions.

Fry the bacon and vegetables until golden brown, and add to the casserole.

Stir the flour into the remaining fat in the frying pan and cook to make a roux.

Gradually stir in the stock.

Bring to the boil and simmer, still stirring, until the liquid thickens.

Add the tomato paste and season to taste.

Pour the sauce over the pigeons and vegetables in the casserole.

Cover the dish and cook in a moderate oven for about 1½ hours until the pigeons are tender.

Peel and slice the mushrooms, and add them to the casserole about 20 minutes before the end of the cooking time.

Oven: 325°F/160°C Gas Mark 3

RABBIT PIE

1 prepared rabbit
Seasoned flour
1 leek
1 hard-boiled egg
4 rashers of bacon
1 tablespoon chopped parsley
Salt and pepper
Stock as required
8 oz (225 g) shortcrust or flaky pastry
Beaten egg to glaze

Joint the rabbit, and roll in the seasoned flour.

Wash and chop the leek.

Chop the egg.

Take the rinds off the bacon and chop into pieces.

Put the rabbit, leek, egg, bacon and parsley into a pie dish.

Season to taste.

Half fill the dish with stock.

Roll out the pastry on a floured board and use to cover the
pie.

Make a hole in the centre for the steam to escape.

Decorate with leaves made from the pastry trimings.

Brush with beaten egg.

Bake in a hot oven for 15 minutes until the pastry is set.

Reduce the temperature to moderate, and continue cooking
for about 1¼ hours or until the filling is tender.

Oven: 425°F/220°C Gas Mark 7

Reduce to: 325°F/160°C Gas Mark 3

IRISH STEW

Long slow cooking is the secret of any stew, and Irish Stew is no exception. Traditionally it would have been made from mutton or kid. The meat would have been left on the bone to improve the flavour, and the vegetables stewed whole. To give authentic Irish flavour the only vegetables added are potatoes and onions, and the meat is not browned first. The dish is accompanied by carrots cooked separately and pickled red cabbage.

**2 lbs (900 g) best end of neck, gigot (sliced leg) or
    shoulder chops
1 lb (450 g) potatoes
4 onions
Salt and pepper
White stock or water to cover
Chopped parsley**

Trim the meat (and cut it into pieces, if preferred).

Peel and slice the potatoes and onions.

If the potatoes are small they can be left whole.

Put the potatoes, onions and meat in layers in a saucepan, seasoning each layer with salt and pepper.

Add the stock or water.

Bring to the boil, and simmer slowly for about 2 hours.

Put the stew in a dish and serve sprinkled with chopped parsley.

SMALL MUTTON PIES

In Graiguenamanagh, County Kilkenny, at the beginning of the century mutton pasties were always made for the Michaelmas Fair on 29th September. It was the biggest sheep fair of the year and farmers from the countryside around started driving in their flocks at dawn. Mutton pies were popular to assuage their hunger when they reached town in the early hours. The pasties were half moon shaped made from baker's dough with yeast in it, and filled with chopped, seasoned mutton. After the custom ceased, they were made as a novelty by Patrick O'Leary's Bakery and these are still remembered. Here is a modern version of small mutton pies.

1 lb (450 g) mutton
2 onions
Chopped parsley
Salt and pepper
A pinch of nutmeg
About ½ pint (300 ml/ 1¼ cups) brown stock
¾ lb (350 g) hot water crust pastry
Beaten egg to glaze

For the hot water crust pastry:
1 lb (450 g) flour
A pinch of salt
4 oz (100 g) lard
½ pint (300 ml/ 1¼ cups) hot water or milk and water

To make the hot water crust pastry:

Sift the flour and slat together into a bowl.

Put the lard into a saucepan with the liquid.

Bring to the boil, and melt the lard in the liquid.

Make a well in the centre of the dry ingredients.

Pour the liquid, quickly mixing to form a soft dough with a wooden spoon.

Knead until quite smooth.

Cover the dough with a plate and leave to rest in a warm for 20 minutes.

To make the small mutton pies:

Mince the mutton.

Peel and chop the onions finely.

Mix the meat with the onions, nutmeg and chopped parsley.

Season to taste, and moisten the mixture with a little of the stock.

Divide the pastry in half.

Keeping the remainder warm, roll out half on a floured board and use to line small tins, or shape into cases using the base of a glass tumbler as a mould.

Fill the pies with the mutton mixture.

Roll out the remaining pastry to make lids, dampening and pressing the edges together to seal.

Make a slit in each pie to allow the steam to escape.

Decorate the edges as required and cut any left over pastry into leaf shapes dampening the underside of the leaves before placing them into position on the pies.

Brush with beaten egg and place the pies on a baking sheet.

Bake in a hot oven for about 10 minutes until the pastry is set.

Reduce the temperature to moderately hot and cook for a further 30 minutes until golden brown.

Warm the remaining stock.

Remove the pies from the oven, and pour the hot stock through the slit in each pie, before serving hot.

Oven: 425°F/220°C Gas Mark 7
Reduce to: 400°F/200°C Gas Mark 6

IRISH BEEF CASSEROLE

1½ lbs (675 g) stewing steak
2 onions
4 oz (100 g) mushrooms
1 oz (25 g) fat for frying
1 oz (25 g) flour
½ pint (300 ml/ 1¼ cups) brown stock
½ pint (300 ml/ 1¼ cups) Guinness
Salt and pepper
Bouquet garni

Trim the steak, and cut in into cubes.

Peel and slice the onions and mushrooms.

Heat the fat in a frying pan and fry the meat to seal on all sides.

Stir in the flour.

Mix the stock and the Guinness together.

Slowly add the stock to the pan, stirring continuously.

Bring to the boil, still stirring. Reduce to a simmer, season with salt and pepper to taste, and add the sliced onions.

Put the mixture into a casserole dish and cook in a moderate oven for 2 hours. (If preferred, cooking can be continued in the saucepan for the same time).

30 minutes before the end of the cooking time add the sliced mushrooms.

Oven: 325°F/160°C Gas Mark 3

SAVOURY MINCED BEEF

Serves 4

2 onions
4 carrots
¼ lb (100 g) mushrooms
1 lb (450 g) minced beef
1 oz (25 g) flour
1 pint (600 ml/ 2½ cups) brown stock
2 tablespoons of tomato purée
Salt and pepper

Peel and slice the onions, carrots and mushrooms.

Put the meat in a large saucepan and cook over a gentle heat until any fat runs out.

Strain this off.

Stir the flour into the meat, and cook for a few minutes.

Gradually add the stock, stirring.

Bring the boil, add the onions, carrots, tomato purée and seasoning.

Simmer for about 1 hour until the meat and vegetables are cooked.

About 20 minutes before the end of the cooking time add the sliced mushrooms.

CORNED BEEF

In Ireland most butchers sell ready-prepared and salted joints of brisket and silverside. To make corned beef or salt beef at home allow about a week before the meat is ready. Pork can also be salted using this method.

For the pickling liquid:
2 pints (1.15 litres/ 4 cups) water
½ lb (225 g) coarse salt
2 oz (50 g) brown sugar
1 teaspoon saltpetre
A bay leaf
½ teaspoon whole cloves
½ teaspoon all spice
½ teaspoon peppercorns

For the corned beef:

1 joint of brisket or silverside weighing about 4 lbs (1.75 kg).

Sufficient common salt to cover.

To make the pickling liquid:

Boil all the ingredients together, removing any scum that forms, and simmering until the liquid is clear.

Allow to cool completely.

To make the corned beef:

Rub the salt into the meat.

Put the joint into a large bowl and completely cover with the pickling liquid

Cover with a plate that will fit inside the bowl and weight this down.

Turn every day for three days.

Rub the meat again with salt.

Replace in the pickling liquid and leave for a further four days, turning occasionally.

CORNED BEEF AND CABBAGE   Serves 4

This is a very famous Irish dish. Butchers tend to pickle brisket and silverside. The process changes the colour of the beef from brown to dark pink.

2 lbs (900 g) corned beef - salt bisket or silverside
Fresh herbs, preferably a sprig of thyme and parsley
3 carrots
2 onions
Pepper
1 green cabbage

If the beef is very salty, soak it for 2 hours in cold water.

Drain and put the meat into a large saucepan.

Cover with fresh cold water.

Peel and slice the carrots and onions.

Bring the meat to the boil and add the carrots, onions and herbs.

Season with pepper to taste and simmer for 1-2 hours, until the meat is tender.

Remove the outer leaves from the cabbage and cut it into quarters. Add the cabbage to the saucepan.

Return the pan to the boil, and then simmer for a further 30 minutes.

Serve the meat surrounded by the cabbage, and vegetables, accompanied by hot Parsley Sauce (see recipe) and mustard.

IRISH SPICED BEEF   Serves 4-6

Spiced Beef is a popular dish at Christmas time in Ireland. It was often eaten cold after midnight on Christmas Eve when the fast ended and the preparations for the Christmas Day festivities were completed. It is sold in butchers' shops during the festive season, often decorated with red ribbon and holly. Beef can be spiced at home, but allow a week for preparation.

4 lbs (1.75 kg) brisket or silverside

For the pickling liquid:
2 shallots
2 bay leaves
½ teaspoon powdered cloves
½ teaspoon mace
2 tablespoon brown sugar
1 teaspoon saltpetre
½ lb (225 g) sea salt

For the Irish Spiced Beef:
The 4 lbs (1.75 kg) brisket or silverside, now spiced
2 carrots
2 onions
Sprigs of fresh mixed herbs
Water
½ pint (300 ml/ 1¼ cups) Guinness

To spice the beef:

Chop the shallots and the bay leaves.

Mix the cloves, mace, brown sugar, saltpetre and sea salt with the shallots and bay leaves.

Rub the mixture thoroughly into the meat.

Place the joint in a large bowl.

If any seasoning mixture is left over, put it in the bottom of the bowl underneath the meat.

Leave in a cool place for one week.

Turn the meat and rub in the seasoning daily.

To make the Irish Spiced Beef:

Peel and slice the carrots and onions.

Put the vegetables in a saucepan with the mixed herbs.

Tie the meat securely, put it in the saucepan.

Cover with warm water.

Bring to the boil, and simmer gently for 2-3 hours until tender.

About one hour before the end of the cooking time add the Guinness.

Put the hot Spiced Beef on a plate or board, cover with another, and weight down until meat is cold.

Carve into slices and eat cold with Pickled Red Cabbage (see recipe).

GAELIC STEAK WITH
IRISH WHISKEY SAUCE

Serves 2

2 oz (50 g) butter or margarine
2 fillet steaks
4 tablespoons cream
4 tablespoons Irish whiskey
Salt and freshly ground black pepper
Oil for frying
Parsley to garnish
Fried onions (optional)

Trim the steaks and season with salt and pepper.

Melt the butter in a frying pan.

Fry the steaks on both sides, for 4-5 minutes.

Remove the meat and keep hot.

Stir in the cream and Irish whiskey into the pan.

Simmer rapidly.

Pour the sauce and the pan juices over the steak.

Garnish with the parsley.

Serve with fried onions.

GAELIC STEAK WITH
IRISH MIST SAUCE

Serves 4

4 sirloin steaks
Salt
Freshly ground black pepper
2 oz (50 g) butter
2 tablespoons Irish Mist liqueur
¼ pint (150 ml/ ⅔ cup) double cream
Watercress for garnish

Trim the steaks and season well with salt and pepper.

Heat the butter in a frying pan.

Fry the steaks for about 5 minutes on each side.

Remove and keep warm.

Stir the cream and Irish Mist liqueur into the pan juices.

Pour the sauce over the steaks.

Serve garnished with watercress.

BAKED LIMERICK HAM

Limerick smoked ham is world famous. Juniper the shrub which grew abundantly in the country, was used in the smoking process. Pork has long been a popular meat in Ireland, and Irish ham and bacon has been justly famous for a long time. In early times a whole pig would be baked in a pit lined with hot stones. In Ireland only the leg of pork is called ham; other cuts are referred to as bacon.

1 Limerick ham weighing about 10 lbs (4.5 kg)
½ glass brandy
½ pint (300 ml/ 1¼ cups) beer
8 oz (225 g) brown sugar
4 oz (100 g) butter
¼ oz (20 g) cloves

As the ham is smoked it should be soaked in cold water for about 12 hours or overnight.

Drain.

Put the ham in a large saucepan, cover with fresh cold water.

Bring slowly to the boil and simmer for 2 hours.

Remove the ham and take off the skin.

Stud the ham with the cloves at regular intervals.

Cream the butter with the sugar and stir in the brandy.

Coat the ham with the mixture.

Place in the oven and bake for about 2½ hours or until golden brown.

Remove and slowly pour the beer over the ham.

Serve hot or cold with Lemon Sauce or Antrim Sauce (see recipe).

Oven: 350°F/180°C Gas Mark 4

PORK AND APPLE STEW

Serves 4

This tasty stew is a traditional favourite in Irish farmhouses.

½ lb (225 g) onions
¾ lb (350 g) cooking apples
4 pork chops
1 oz (25 g) butter or margarine
Salt and black pepper
1 tablespoon brown sugar
¾ pint (450 ml/ 2 cups) brown stock or cider
A pinch of sage

Peel, core and slice the apples.

Peel and slice the onions.

Trim off any excess fat from the chops.

Heat the butter in a frying pan and fry the chops to seal on both sides.

Put a layer of onion and apple slices in the bottom of an ovenproof dish.

Arrange the chops on top.

Season with salt, pepper and sage.

Put another layer of onions and apple slices on top of the chops.

Sprinkle with brown sugar.

Pour on the stock or cider.

Cover the casserole and cook in a moderate oven for about 1½ hours or until the pork is tender.

Oven: 350°F/180°C Gas Mark 4

DUBLIN CODDLE

Serves 4

This is a favourite Saturday night supper in Dublin and there are many versions of the dish. It is said to have been a favourite of Jonathan Swift, 1667-1745, the satirist and author of *Gulliver's Travels*. A cleric, he was appointed Dean of St. Patrick's, Dublin in 1713. Coddle is traditionally made with collar rashers, which have become known as coddle bacon.

½ lb (225 g) Irish bacon rashers
2 onions
1½ lbs (675 g) potatoes
1 lb (450 g) Irish pork sausages
½ pint (300 ml/ 1¼ cups) water
½ pint (300 ml/ 1¼ cups) milk
Salt and pepper
Chopped parsley

Remove the rinds from the rashers and cut into pieces.

Peel and slice the onions.

Peel and slice the potatoes.

Put the bacon, onions, potatoes and sausages into a large saucepan or ovenproof dish.

Season with salt and pepper to taste.

Mix the water and milk together, and pour on sufficient liquid just to cover the ingredients.

Bring to the boil, cover and simmer gently for 1 hour (or bake in a moderate oven) until cooked through and the liquid reduced.

Serve straight from the pot garnished with chopped parsley.

Delicious accompanied by soda bread.

Oven: 350°F/180°C Gas Mark 4

CRUBEENS AND GUINNESS

Serves 4

It is said that "Eating crubeens, alternated with liberal amounts of Guinness, puts oysters in the shade". This old tradition still survives in certain places especially in country pubs and even in Dublin.

Crubeens should always be eaten with the fingers not with a knife and fork.

12 pig trotters (crubeens)
2 onions
2 carrots
A bay leaf
Salt
A bunch of fresh herbs, such as parsley and thyme
1 tablespoon dry mustard

Wash the crubeens and put them into a saucepan of cold water.

Peel and slice the onions and carrots.

Add the vegetables and herbs to the saucepan.

Cover and bring to the boil.

Simmer for 30 minutes.

Pour off the water and add fresh liquid with the mustard.

Bring to the boil again, and simmer for a further 15 minutes or until the meat comes away from the bone.

Drain.

The stock and vegetables make excellent soup.

Serve the crubeens hot or cold.

TRIPE AND ONIONS

Serves 6

Tripe and onions, sometimes on toast, was a popular treat for breakfast on Sundays. It was particularly enjoyed by people returning home after attending early mass, because it could be prepared in advance, and left on top of the stove or in the oven. It was also a favourite for Saturday night supper.

2 lbs (900 g) dressed tripe
1½ lbs (675 g) onions
Salt and pepper
1 pint (600 ml/ 2½ cups) milk
A pinch of nutmeg
1 oz (25 g) flour or cornflour
2 oz (50 g) butter
Chopped parsley to decorate

Cut up the tripe into thin strips.

Peel and slice the onions.

Put the tripe, butter and onions in a saucepan.

Cover with the milk, reserving a very small quantity.

Season with salt and pepper.

Add nutmeg to taste.

Cover and gently bring to the boil.

Cook over a low heat for about 1½-2 hours, stirring occasionally.

Alternatively the tripe can be baked in a casserole in a cool oven for the same time.

Blend the flour or cornflour with the reserved milk, and stir this into the dish.

Continue cooking for a further 10 minutes until thickened.

Serve garnished with chopped parsley.

Oven: 300°F/150°C Gas Mark 2

WHITE PUDDING

These puddings are so called because they contain no blood and therefore differ in colour from black puddings. They are equally good served with a traditional Irish breakfast, or as a main course.

1 lb (450 g) coarse oatmeal
½ lb (225 g) onion
½ lb (225 g) chopped beef suet
Salt and pepper
Prepared purchased sausage skins

Spread the oatmeal on a baking sheet and bake in a slow oven until golden brown.

Peel and chop the onion finely.

Mix the oatmeal and onion with the chopped beef suet.

Season to taste with salt and pepper.

Put the mixture into the sausage skins allowing room for expansion.

Tie both ends of each sausage.

Prick the skins to prevent bursting.

Cook the sausages or puddings in boiling water for about 1 hour, pricking the skins occasionally.

Hang the puddings up in a cool, dry place, where they can be stored for several weeks.

Before serving, boil the puddings again for 15 minutes, or cut them into pieces, brush with beaten egg, dip in breadcrumbs, and fry.

LIVER, BACON AND ONION HOTPOT

Delicious cooked in a casserole, liver can also be rolled in the seasoned flour and fried lightly on both sides in butter or oil with rashers of bacon.

1 lb (450 g) lambs' or calves' liver
A little flour
A pinch of sage
½ lb (225 g) bacon rashers
1 lb (450 g) onions
About ¾ pint (450 ml/ 2 cups) brown stock
Salt and pepper

Wash and dry the liver.

Trim and cut into thin slices.

Season the flour with the sage.

Roll the liver in the flour to coat.

Remove the rinds from the bacon and cut it into pieces.

Peel and slice the onions.

Put layers of liver, bacon and onion in an ovenproof casserole dish.

Pour on the stock to come half way up the casserole.

Season with salt and pepper to taste.

Cover the casserole, and cook in a moderate oven for 2 hours.

Oven: 350°F/180°C Gas Mark 4

CREAMED SWEDES

Swedes are commonly eaten in Ireland during the winter months.
popular vegetable is a member of the turnip family. In the United St
swedes are known as Rutabaga - a name which at one time was used
the vegetable in Ireland. No doubt it was introduced in America by I
people who made their home across the Atlantic.

1 lb (450 g) swedes
Salt and pepper
1 oz (25 g) butter
2 tablespoons cream
A pinch of cinnamon

Peel and cut up the swedes.

Put in a saucepan of cold, salted water.

Bring to the boil and simmer until tender.

Drain and mash.

Beat in the butter.

Season well with pepper.

Add the cinnamon, and stir in the cream.

Serve hot.

COLCANNON

Serves 6

The name Colcannon comes from *cal ceann fhionn,* which means white
headed cabbage, though the dish is also made from kale nowadays. It was
always served on All Hallows' Day, 31st October, which was a fast day for
many centuries past, when no meat could be eaten. As it happens the dish
is very good served with cold meat.

1 lb (450 g) potatoes
Salt and pepper
1 lb (450 g) white cabbage or kale
2½ fl oz (4 tablespoons/ ⅓ cup) milk
2½ fl oz (4 tablespoons/ ⅓ cup) cream
1 onion or 6 spring onions
4 oz (100 g) butter
Chopped parsley

Peel and boil the potatoes in salted water until soft.

Drain and mash well with half the butter.

Cook the cabbage or kale in boiling salted water until tender.

Drain well, and chop.

Peel and chop or mince the onion finely; or trim and chop
the spring onions.

Add the onions to the milk.

Bring to the boil and simmer until tender.

Allow to cool a little, then add the cream.

Add the cooked cabbage or kale, onions and milk to the
potatoes. Season with pepper, and more salt if required.

Beat well together over the stove, taking care not to let the
Colcannon brown.

Put the mixture into a warmed vegetable dish.

Melt the rest of the butter and pour it into a well in the centre
of the Colcannon before serving garnished with chopped
parsley.

CHAMP OR POUNDIES

Serves 2-3

Possibly the most popular of all the favourite potato dishes in Ireland, champ is often served on Fridays during Lent. It is usually eaten with a spoon. Champ can also be made with chopped parsley, chives, young nettle tops or freshly cooked peas. A little cream may be added as well. Scrambled eggs in the centre of the dish make an attractive lunch or supper dish.

1 lb (450 g) potatoes
8 spring onions (or to taste) or 1 onion
4 fl oz (6 tablespoon/ ½ cup) milk
2 oz (50 g) butter
Salt and pepper

Peel and slice the potatoes and simmer in a saucepan of salted water until tender.

Drain, and mash well and keep hot.

Chop the spring onions using the green as well as the white parts or peel and chop the onion.

Cook the chopped onions in the milk until soft.

Beat the hot milk, onions and pepper into the potatoes.

The mixture should be soft and fluffy but not sloppy.

Pile into a warm serving dish.

Make a hole in the centre and put in the butter.

POTATOES IN CHIVE CREAM

FROM BALLYMAKEIGH HOUSE

Ser

1½ lbs (675 g) small potatoes - peeled
¾ pint (450 ml/ 2 cups) cream
4 tablespoons chives, finely chopped
Salt and pepper

Steam the potatoes until tender.

In a separate saucepan combine the cream, chives a seasoning.

Simmer the mixture for 5 minutes.

Put the potatoes into the chive cream.

Reheat and serve.

POTATO DUMPLINGS

Potato dumplings make a tasty and nourishing addition to any stew or soup.

About ½ cup flour
¾ teaspoon baking powder
A pinch of salt
1 cup mashed potato

Sieve the flour with the baking powder and salt.

Mix sufficient flour with the mashed potato to make a stif dough.

Knead lightly, and mould the mixture into a long roll.

Slice the roll into ½ inch (1 cm) slices.

Add the slices to any stew or soup about 20 minutes befo the end of cooking time.

BAKED ONIONS

Serves 4

Second only to the potato, onions are a very popular vegetable in Ireland.
As well as being used in soups and stews, they can also be baked, as here.
Alternatively onions can be baked by peeling and parboiling before roasting
in the same tin as the joint for the last hour of cooking time, and basting
frequently.

4 large onions, unpeeled
Salt and pepper
4 knobs of butter

Place the unpeeled onions in an ovenproof dish with a little
water. This should be no more then 1 inch (2.5 cm) in depth.

Bake in a moderate oven for about 1½ hours, or until the
onions are soft and nicely cooked.

Peel off the outer skin of each onion and cut off at the base.

Sprinkle the vegetables with salt and pepper.

Just before serving top each onion with a knob of butter.

Oven: 325°F/160°C Gas Mark 3

BREAD AND BUTTER PUDDING   Serves 4

This delicious pudding can be made with stale bread, which made it very popular during hard times. It can be spiced with nutmeg, mixed spice or even a drop of rum.

4 large slices of stale bread
1½ oz (40 g) butter or margarine
3 oz (75 g) sugar
3 oz (75 g) sultanas
2 eggs
½ pint (300 ml/ 1¼ cups) milk
1 oz (25 g) sugar for the top
A pinch of nutmeg

Cut the crusts from the bread and butter each slice.

Cut the bread into large pieces.

Cover the bottom of a greased (2 pint/ 1 litre) pie dish with a layer of bread, buttered side up.

Sprinkle with sugar and sultanas.

Put another layer of bread, sugar and sultanas and final layer of bread on top, buttered side down.

Beat the eggs with the milk.

Pour the egg mixture over the bread and leave the dish to stand for at least ½ hour.

Sprinkle the top with sugar and nutmeg.

Bake in a moderately hot oven for about an hour.

Oven: 350°F/180°C Gas Mark 4 for about 1 hour

PARTEEN PUDDING

Parteen is a country village close to Limerick in County Clare. The County is renowned for its music and set-dancing. The people are also partial to a sweet pudding like this one which is named after the village of Parteen.

4 oz (100 g) plain flour
1 teaspoon baking powder
1 teaspoon mixed spice
2 oz (50 g) breadcrumbs
6 oz (175 g) sugar
4 oz (100 g) shredded suet
4 oz (100 g) sultanas
4 oz (100 g) mixed dried fruit
6 oz (175 g) grated apple
4 oz (100 g) grated carrots
4 tablespoons sherry

Combine the dry ingredients.

Add the sherry, mixing well, to moisten the mixture.

Grease a round pudding basin.

Fill with the mixture leaving room at the top for the pudding to rise.

Cover the basin with greaseproof paper securely tied.

Steam the pudding in a pan of boiling water for about 3 hours.

Do no allow the pan to boil dry.

CARRAGHEEN PUDDING

Carragheen is a nutritious, edible moss rich in iodine and other sea salts. It is found on the rocks of the west coast of Ireland at low tide. It is gathered in April and May and if bleached and dried will keep indefinitely. It has many culinary uses from drinks to delicious puddings and acts as gelatine. It is also renowned for its medical and health giving qualities. Carragheen moss can be obtained in health food shops but should be soaked before use.

½ oz (15 g) Carragheen Moss
1½ pints (900ml/ 3¾ cups) milk
Grated rind of one lemon
2 oz (50 g) sugar
Whipped cream for decoration
Fresh or stewed fruit if desired

Wash the moss and leave it to soak in cold water for 15 minutes.

Drain well.

Put the moss in a saucepan with the milk and the lemon rind.

Bring to the boil and cook until a small amount will set when put on a saucer.

Stir in the sugar and pour into a wetted mould.

Chill and leave to set.

Turn out of the mould.

Surround the pudding with whipped cream.

The dish can be served with fresh fruit slices or stewed fruit such as apples, rhubarb or blackberries.

CHOCOLATE CARRAGHEEN SOUFFLÉ

Serves 4

½ oz (15 g) Carragheen moss
1 pint (600 ml/ 2½ cups) milk
1 oz (25 g) cocoa
1 egg, separated
2 oz (50 g) sugar
¼ pint (150 ml/ ⅔ cup) double cream
Grated chocolate and chopped nuts for decoration

Soak the moss in cold water overnight.

Drain well.

Blend the cocoa with a little of the milk.

Put the moss, cocoa and remaining milk in a pan and bring to the boil.

Simmer until the mixture begins to thicken.

Remove from the heat.

Mix the egg yolk with the sugar and pour over the strained moss and chocolate mixture.

Return to the pan and contine cooking for a few more minutes, stirring continuously.

Allow to cool a little.

Fold in the stiffly beaten egg white and the whipped cream.

Pour into individual glass dishes or a serving dish.

Leave to set in a cold place or refrigerator.

Decorate with grated chocolate swirls and chopped nuts.

HONEY APPLE TART

Honey was commonly used to sweeten fruit.

8 oz (225 g) shortcrust pastry
3-4 good sized cooking apples
2 tablespoons Irish honey

Roll out the pastry on a floured surface.

Reserve a little pastry for decoration and use the rest to line a greased flan tin.

Peel, core and slice the apples.

Put in a pan with the honey and cook over a very gently heat until the fruit is just soft.

Arrange the fruit in the prepared flan case.

Cut the remaining pastry in narrow strips and use for decoration across the top of the flan.

Bake in a moderately hot oven for about 20 minutes or until the pastry is golden brown.

Oven: 400°F/200°C Gas Mark 6

APPLE SOUFFLE CHEESECAKE Serves 10-12

For the biscuit base:
4 oz (100 g) melted butter
6 oz (175 g) ginger biscuits, crushed

For the filling:
1 lb (450 g) cooking apples, peeled cored and sliced
  or ½ pint (300 ml/ 1¼ cups) apple purée
5 tablespoons water
½ oz (15 g) sachet of gelatine
8 oz (225 g) cottage cheese, sieved
¼ pint (150 ml/ ⅔ cup) soured cream
6 oz (175 g) caster sugar
2 eggs, separated
Whipped cream or apple slices to decorate, optional

Stir together the melted butter and biscuit crumbs.

Press into the base of 9 inch (23 cm) greased-bottomed cake or deep flan tin. Chill.

If using fresh apples, cook in 3 tablespoons of water on a low heat until soft.

Put 2 tablespoons water in a small heatproof dish, sprinkle over the gelatine and leave to soak for 2 minutes.

Stand the dish in a pan of hot water until the gelatine is completely dissolved.

In a large bowl, mix the cottage cheese, soured cream, apple purée, sugar and beaten egg yolks.

Stir in dissolved gelatine.

Whisk egg whites until stiff and fold them into the mixture.

Pour over the prepared biscuit crumb base and chill until set.

When set, turn out and decorate with whipped cream or apple slices.

STRAWBERRY CURD CHEESECAKE

Serves 6-8

Strawberries are grown extensively in the south east of Ireland. In the height of the summer strawberry sellers can be found on the road sides and ladies sell cartfuls of strawberries in the streets of Dublin city. Cheesecakes were originally made with curd cheese.

For the base:
8 oz (225 g) shortcrust pastry, chilled

For the filling:
1 lb (450 g) curd cheese
6 oz (175 g) sugar
2 eggs, separated
1 teaspoon vanilla essence

For the topping:
½ lb (225 g) fresh strawberries
½ pint (300 ml/ 1¼ cups) double cream, whipped

Mix the curd cheese with the egg yolks and sugar and beat to a smooth cream.

Beat the egg whites until they are stiff.

Fold into the cheese mixture and add the vanilla essence.

Roll our the previously chilled pastry on a floured surface.

Line a greased 8 inch (20 cm) flan tin with the pastry.

Pour in the curd cheese mixture.

Bake in a moderately hot oven for about 30-40 minutes.

Remove from the oven and allow to cool at room temperature.

Top with a layer of whipped cream.

Wash and hull the strawberries and decorate the top of the cake with the fruit. Serve immediately.

Oven: 350°F/180°C Gas Mark 4 for 30 minutes.

ORANGE MOUSSE

Serves 4-6

½ pint (300 ml/ 1¼ cups) orange juice
3 oz (75 g) caster sugar
4 oz (100 g) sachet of gelatine
3 fl oz (4½/ tablespoons) cointreau
1 egg white
½ pint (300 ml/ 1¼ cups) whipping cream
1 packet of Boudoir biscuits
Mandarin oranges
¼ pint (150 ml/ ⅔ cup) whipped cream for decoration,
   optional

Heat the orange juice and sugar in a pan, but do not boil.

Sprinkle in the gelatine, stir well, then leave until the liquid is cold.

Add the cointreau.

Beat the egg white until stiff.

Whip the cream until thick and fold in the beaten egg white.

Stir in the orange mixture.

Leave the mixture until nearly set for about 1-1½ hours.

Halve the boudoir biscuits and use to line the edge of an 8 inch (20 cm) or 9 inch (23 cm) loose-bottomed tin.

Pour the orange mixture into the tin.

Leave the mousse in the fridge until it is set.

Remove from the tin and decorate with mandarin oranges and whipped cream if liked.

APPLE PIE

The Irish apple pie is more like a covered tart as it is baked on a flat tin plate. Other seasonal fruits such as gooseberries and rhubarb also make excellent fillings.

12 oz (350 g) flour
A pinch of salt
12 oz (350 g) butter or margarine
A little milk
4 large cooking apples
3 oz (75 g) sugar
3 or 4 cloves
Caster sugar for dusting

Sieve the flour with the salt into a mixing bowl.

Rub the fat into the flour until it resembles fine breadcrumbs.

Add enough milk to form a stiff dough.

Leave the dough to stand at room temperature for about an hour.

Roll out half the pastry onto a floured surface.

Cut out a circle large enough to cover a 10 inch (25 cm) plate.

Grease the plate with butter and line with the pastry.

Peel, core and finely slice the apples.

Pour a tablespoon of water over the apples and sprinkle with sugar.

Add the cloves.

Roll out the remaining pastry and use to cover the pie.

Dampen the edges with water and press well together.

Trim any excess pastry and make 2 small cuts in the centre.

Sprinkle with caster sugar.

Bake in a moderately hot oven for about 45 minutes or until the pastry is golden brown.

Oven: 400°F/200°C Gas Mark 6

RICE PUDDING

1½ pints (900ml/ 3¾ cups) milk
2 oz (50 g) pudding rice
2 oz (50 g) sugar
½ oz (15 g) butter
1 teaspoon ground nutmeg

Grease a pie dish.

Wash the rice and put into the dish.

Pour over the milk and add the sugar, stir to mix.

Dot pieces of butter over the top and sprinkle with nutmeg.

Leave to stand for at least ½ an hour.

Bake in a moderate oven for 2 hours.

Oven: 325°F/160°C Gas Mark 3 for 2 hours.

SWEET BLACK PUDDING

Serves 4-6

4 oz (100 g) breadcrumbs
4 oz (100 g) suet
1 teaspoon of mixed spice
3 oz (75 g) currants
3 oz (75 g) raisins
2 oz (50 g) ground almonds
6 oz (175 g) sugar
2 eggs, separated
½ pint (300 ml/ 1¼ cups) cream
1 tablespoon brandy

Mix the breadcrumbs, suet and spice together.

Add the fruit, almonds and sugar, mixing well.

Beat the egg yolks, cream and brandy, and stir into the mixture.

Fold in the stiffly beaten egg whites.

Put the mixture into a greased pudding basin.

Cover with greaseproof paper, securely tied.

Steam for 3 hours in a pan of boiling water.

Top up the pan with water during cooking.

Do not allow to boil dry.

Pudding

CHRISTMAS PLUM PUDDING

Serves 6-8

8 oz (225 g) flour
A pinch of salt
1 teaspoon baking powder
2 teaspoons mixed spice
8 oz (225 g) breadcrumbs
8 oz (225 g) suet
6 oz (175 g) brown sugar
14 oz (575 g) mixed dried fruit
2 oz (50 g) cherries, halved
2 oz (50 g) candied peel
2 oz (50 g) almonds, chopped
2 eggs, beaten
2 tablespoons treacle
½ glass brandy
A little milk

Sift together the flour, salt, baking powder and spice.

Add the breadcrumbs, suet and sugar, mixing the ingredients well together.

Add the mixed fruit, cherries, candied peel and almonds.

Add the beaten eggs, treacle, brandy and enough milk necessary to make a soft pudding mixture.

Blend the ingredients thoroughly.

Grease a pudding basin and fill with the mixture allowing a little space at the top of the basin for the pudding to rise.

Cover the basin with 2 sheets of greaseproof paper, securely tied.

Steam in a pan of boiling water for about 5 hours. Do not allow the pan to boil dry. Top up the water in the pan regularly.

Serve flaming with brandy or whiskey and decorated with a sprig of holly.

STEAMED FIG PUDDING   Serves 4-6

6 oz (175 g) figs
4 oz (100 g) self-raising flour
4 oz (100 g) breadcrumbs
4 oz (100 g) suet
A pinch of salt
1 teaspoon cinnamon
6 oz (175 g) sugar
1 egg, beaten
1 tablespoon honey
A little milk

Soak the figs in cold water and leave overnight.

Mix together the flour, breadcrumbs and suet.

Add a pinch of salt and the cinnamon.

Stir in the sugar and the drained and chopped figs.

Blend in the egg and honey.

Add sufficient milk to make a soft dropping consistency.

Put the mixture into a greased pudding basin - no more than three quarters full to allow the pudding to rise.

Cover with greaseproof paper and tie securely.

Steam the pudding in a pan of boiling water for about 3 hours.

Do not allow the pan to boil dry.

POTATO APPLE PUDDING

8 oz (225 g) flour
½ teaspoon baking powder
A good pinch of salt
½ teaspoon of ground ginger
2 oz (50 g) butter, melted
8 oz (225 g) mashed potato
A little milk
4 large cooking apples
2 oz (50 g) sugar
2-3 cloves to taste
A little lemon juice

Sift together the flour, baking powder, salt and ground ginger.

Mix the melted butter with the mashed potatoes.

Add the flour mixture and knead lightly into a soft dough, adding a little milk if necessary.

Roll out the pastry on a floured surface to a ½ inch (1 cm) thickness.

Line a greased pudding basin with the pastry, reserving enough to make a lid.

Peel, core and slice the apples.

Fill the basin with the apples, sprinkle with sugar and add cloves to taste. Squeeze a little lemon juice over the apple.

Cover the pudding with a pastry lid, dampening the edges to seal the pastry.

Securely cover with greaseproof paper foil.

Steam the pudding in a pan of boiling water for 2½ hours. and do not allow it to boil dry.

Turn out and serve the pudding in wedges with a custard or wine sauce or whipped cream.

IRISH POTATO BREAD OR FADGE

Irish Potato Bread (potato cake), also called Fadge, is lovely served hot, split and buttered. Alternatively it can be served with bacon and sausages by frying in bacon fat until brown on both sides.

1 lb (450 g) of cooked mashed potatoes
1 oz (25 g) butter or margarine
1 teaspoon salt
4 oz (100 g) flour

Preferably while the potatoes are still warm, add the flour, butter and salt.

Work in the flour using the minimum necessary to make a stiff dough.

Roll out to about ½ inch thick and cut into triangles.

Cook on a hot floured griddle or in a frying pan until golden brown on both sides.

ROCK CAKES

These cakes are delicious served hot for tea. They will also keep very well if allowed to cool and stored in an airtight container.

8 oz (225 g) flour
½ teaspoon salt
1 teaspoon baking powder
2 oz (50 g) butter or margarine
3 oz (75 g) granulated sugar
3 oz (75 g) currants
1 egg, beaten
Grated rind of ½ lemon
1 or 2 tablespoons of milk

Sieve the flour and salt together into a mixing bowl.

Add the baking powder and salt.

Rub in the butter or margarine until the mixture resembles fine breadcrumbs.

Mix in the sugar and fruit.

Add the beaten egg.

Add the grated lemon rind and enough milk to make a stiff, dough.

Prepare a greased baking sheet.

Spoon drops of the cake mixture onto the sheet and bake in a moderately hot oven for about 20 minutes.

Oven: 400°F/200°C Gas Mark 6

OATMEAL CAKES

This is a very old recipe for oatmeal cakes which has been handed down through the generations. A lady with very big hands who gave the recipe to Jean McKean of The Hall Greene Farm Guest House, Lifford, County Donegal, showed her the quantities in handfuls! Mrs. McKean has since weighed out the amounts. These oatmeal cakes are very popular with her guests - particularly those from overseas - as is the rest of Jean McKean's delicious home-made fare. The oatcakes are best made with coarse oatmeal, and keep very well in an airtight container.

6 oz (175 g) plain flour
5 oz (150 g) oatmeal
2 oz (50 g) sugar
3 oz (75 g) margarine
A pinch of baking powder
A pinch of salt
A little hot water

Sieve the flour, salt and baking powder into a bowl.

Rub in the fat.

Add the sugar and mix in the oatmeal.

Add sufficient hot water to bind the mixture together. Do not allow the dough to be too soft.

Roll out the dough on a floured surface to ½ inch (1 cm) thickness and make diamond shapes by cutting diagonally out of a strip of pastry.

Place on a floured baking tray in a moderately hot oven for 25 minutes turning half way through cooking.

Serve buttered, with jam, honey or cheese.

Oven: 375°F/190°C Gas Mark 5

WEXFORD BROWNIES

These rich and sticky fingers are a favourite with children.

4 oz (100 g) butter or margarine
8 oz (225 g) brown sugar
2 eggs, beaten
1 teaspoon vanilla essence
4 oz (100 g) plain flour
A pinch of salt
2 teaspoons baking powder
4 oz (100 g) chopped walnuts

Melt the butter with the sugar in a pan over a gentle heat.

Allow to cool.

Stir in the eggs and the vanilla essence.

Add the flour, salt, baking powder and walnuts.

Mix together thoroughly.

Grease and line an 11 inch (28 cm) x 7 inch (18 cm) swiss roll tin.

Pour in the mixture and bake in a moderate oven for about 20 minutes.

Remove from the oven and allow to cool.

When almost cold cut the cake into fingers.

The brownies will keep well in an air-tight container.

Oven: 325°F/160°C Gas Mark 3

HALL GREENE COOKIES

A modern recipe for a traditional biscuit, this is a prize winning recipe from Mrs. Jean McKean of Hall Greene Farm Guest House in Lifford, County Donegal.

6 oz (175 g) flour
1 teaspoon baking soda
1 teaspoon baking powder
6 oz (175 g) caster sugar
4 oz (100 g) butter
4 oz (100 g) cookeen
1 egg
4 oz (100 g) flakemeal or rolled oats
2 oz (50 g) crushed weetabix
3 oz (75 g) cornflakes or branflakes
2 oz (50 g) coconut
2 oz (50 g) demerara sugar

Sieve the flour, soda and baking powder.

Cream together the sugar and fats.

Add the egg and mix well.

Fold in the flour.

Add the cereals and the coconut, mixing well.

Shape into small balls and roll each one in the demerara sugar.

Place the rounds on a greased baking tray.

Bake in a moderately hot oven until golden brown.

Cool on a wire tray and store in an airtight container.

Oven: 350°F/180°C Gas Mark 4

PORTER CAKE

A traditional Irish cake which used to be made with Porter, a weak stout. Porter was a popular working man's drink but it is no longer produced. Guinness, which is now preferred, is stronger stout and also excellent for making this cake.

1 lb (450 g) flour
A pinch of salt
A teaspoon of baking powder
1 teaspoon of mixed spice
½ lb (225 g) butter
8 oz (225 g) brown sugar
1 teaspoon nutmeg
1 lb (450 g) mixed dried fruit such as raisins, currants, sultanas
The grated rind of 1 lemon
2 eggs, beaten
½ pint (300 ml/ 1¼ cups) Stout or Guinness

Sieve the flour with the salt into a mixing bowl.

Mix the baking powder, sugar and spice.

Rub in the butter.

Add the dried fruit, mixing thoroughly.

Mix the stout with the beaten eggs and blend into the cake mixture.

Grease and line a 8 inch (20 cm) cake tin.

Pour in the mixture and bake in a moderately hot oven for 2 hours or until a skewer comes out clean from the centre of the cake.

Allow to cool in the tin.

This cake is best wrapped up or covered in foil and left for a few days before eating.

Oven: 375°F/190°C Gas Mark 5

POTATO APPLE CAKE

Serves 4

Potato Apple Cake is a traditional Irish cake made with potato cake dough instead of pastry. It would be eaten during apple harvest time and was also a speciality on Halloween with the addition of a wedding ring wrapped up inside it. It was the custom to put a ring into special food on Halloween, and it was said that whoever has the slice with the ring will be wed within a year.

Potato apple cake makes an excellent pudding. After the initial cooking, the cake is split, spread with butter, sugar and cinnamon, which is melted to make a delicious sauce.

1 lb (450 g) mashed potatoes
2 oz (50 g) butter
4 oz (100 g) flour
A pinch of salt
½ teaspoon baking powder
3-4 apples
2 tablespoons sugar
1 oz (25 g) butter
½ teaspoon cinnamon

Mix the butter into the freshly mashed potatoes.

Sift the flour with the salt and baking powder.

Add the flour to the mashed potatoes and work to a pliable dough.

Divide and roll out the dough on a floured surface into 2 circles. Place one circle on a greased baking tray.

Peel, core and slice the apples.

Cover the pastry circle with the raw apple slices.

Dampen the edges and put the other circle on top, pressing together to seal the edges.

Bake in a moderately hot oven for 30-40 minutes or until golden brown.

Remove from the oven and carefully remove the upper pastry crust.

Sprinkle the apples with sugar and cinnamon and dot with butter.

Replace the top and return to the oven for a few minutes to allow the sauce to melt.

Serve whilst hot.

Oven: 375°F/190°C Gas Mark 5

RINK CAKE

A traditional cake which was served at Irish dances.

4 oz (100 g) plain flour
1 teaspoon baking powder
A pinch of salt
2 oz (50 g) butter
4 oz (100 g) caster sugar
2 eggs, beaten
2 oz (50 g) blanched almonds, chopped
3 oz (75 g) currants

Sift together the flour, baking powder and salt.

Rub in the butter until the mixture resembles fine breadcrumbs.

Add the sugar.

Blend in the eggs.

Grease a shallow cake tin.

Pour in the mixture and cover the top with almonds and raisins.

Bake in a moderately hot oven for 20-25 minutes.
Oven: 375°F/190°C Gas Mark 5

WHOLEMEAL HONEY BISCUITS

Makes about 12 biscuits

8 oz (225 g) wholemeal flour
1 teaspoon baking powder
A pinch of salt
4 oz (100 g) butter
2 oz (50 g) sugar
1 egg
2 or 3 tablespoons of honey

Cream together the butter and the sugar.

Beat the egg.

Add the baking powder and salt to the flour and fold into the mixture.

Knead to a smooth dough.

Flour a board with wholemeal flour and roll out the dough.

Cut into 2 inch (5 cm) rounds.

Warm the honey until it melts and brush over each biscuit.

Place the biscuits on a greased baking tray and bake in a moderately hot oven for 15-20 minutes.

Oven: 375°F/190°C Gas Mark 5 for 15-20 minutes.

ORANGE ICED GINGERBREAD

For the gingerbread:
8 oz (225 g) flour
1 teaspoon baking powder
2 teaspoons ground ginger
4 oz (100 g) butter or margarine
3 oz (75 g) golden syrup
3 oz (75 g) treacle
2 oz (50 g) soft brown sugar
2 eggs, well beaten
¼ pint (150 ml/ ⅔ cup) milk

For the icing:
8 oz (225 g) icing sugar
The juice of an orange
A little warm water to mix

Sift the flour into a bowl with the baking powder and ginger.

Melt the butter and the syrup, treacle and sugar in a pan.

Blend into the flour.

Add the beaten eggs and the milk.

Grease and line a square cake tin.

Pour in the mixture and bake in a moderate oven for about 1½ hours or until firm.

Leave in the tin to cool, then cut into squares.

To make the icing:

Sift the icing sugar into a mixing bowl.

Stir in the orange juice and a little warm water if necessary to make a thick icing.

Spread the icing over each gingerbread and decorate with a piece of crystallized ginger.

Oven: 325°F/160°C Gas Mark 3

CHRISTMAS CAKE

This cake is best made 3-4 weeks before eating. It should be stored in an airtight container. Extra whiskey can be poured over the cake before covering with almond paste and icing.

10 oz (275 g) mixed fruit
2 oz (50 g) cherries, halved
2 oz (50 g) almonds, chopped
½ glass Irish whiskey
Rind and juice of 1 lemon
6 oz (175 g) butter
6 oz (175 g) sugar
3 eggs
8 oz (225 g) flour
1 teaspoon mixed spice

Mix the fruit, lemon and almonds with the whiskey and leave in a warm place for at least 2-3 hours, or preferably the night before preparing the cake.

Cream the butter and sugar together.

Add the eggs one at a time with a tablespoon of flour.

Fold in the remaining flour and spices.

Add the fruit and whiskey and mix.

Grease and line a cake tin and pour in the mixture.

Bake in a moderate oven for 2-2½ hours. Test with a skewer and if it leaves the cake clean the cooking is complete.

HALLOWEEN BRACK OR BARNBRACK

Ireland's most famous cakes were originally called Barnbrack, meaning speckled cakes. Barnbrack is traditionally served at tea time on Halloween with a strong 'cuppa'. On this occasion the brack is made with a wedding ring wrapped up with paper and put inside the cake mixture prior to baking and, according to legend, whoever receives the slice with the wedding ring will be married within the year.

Barnbrack is a yeast cake, barm or barn, being the old word for yeast. Bracks made with tea, like this, are also still popular.

½ pint (300 ml/ 1¼ cups) of black tea
12 oz (350 g) brown sugar
8 oz (225 g) raisins
8 oz (225 g) sultanas
2 oz (50 g) butter or margarine
1 large egg, beaten
2 oz (50 g) cherries, chopped
2 oz (50 g) candied peel
1 oz (25 g) almonds chopped
10 oz (275 g) flour
1 heaped teaspoon baking powder

Dissolve the sugar in the tea.

Add the raisins and sultanas and leave to stand overnight.

Melt the butter and mix in with the beaten egg, cherries, candied peel and almonds.

Sieve the flour and add to the mixture with the baking powder, mixing thoroughly.

Grease an 8 inch (20 cm) cake tin and turn in the mixture.

If wished, at this point the wedding ring or silver coin, well wrapped in buttered paper, can be dropped in.

Bake in a moderate oven for 1½ hours.

Oven: 350°F/180°C Gas Mark 4

CHEESE SCONES

Makes about 18 scones

FROM BALLYMAKEIGH HOUSE

1 lb (450 g) plain white flour
3 teaspoons baking powder
2 oz (50 g) butter
2 teaspoons dried mixed herbs
1 teaspoon mustard
Salt and pepper
4 oz (100 g) strong cheddar cheese, grated
1 egg
7 fl oz (200 ml/ ¾ cup) milk
A little parmesan cheese
1 egg yolk, beaten for glazing

Mix the flour with the baking powder.

Rub the fat into the flour until it forms a fine breadcrumb mixture.

Add the dry ingredients.

Mix in the grated cheddar cheese.

Whisk the egg with the milk and add to the mixture.

Knead lightly to form a soft dough.

Roll out on a floured board to about ½ inch (1 cm) thick.

Cut 2 inch (5 cm) rounds and place on a greased baking tray.

Brush the top of each scone with egg yolk.

Sprinkle a litte parmesan cheese on each scone and bake in a moderately hot oven for 20-25 minutes.

Oven: 400°F/200°C Gas Mark 6

MAMMY'S BROWN BUNS Makes about 12 buns

This is an old family recipe for Wheaten buns. They were so popular that the son of the house took eight of them to school for lunch everyday.

4 oz (100 g) plain flour
4 oz (100 g) wheatmeal or wholemeal
2 oz (50 g) bran
1 heaped teaspoon bicarbonate of soda
½ teaspoon salt
½-¾ pint (300 ml/ 1¼ cups - 450 ml/ 2 cups)
buttermilk or sour milk

Mix together the dry ingredients.

Add the liquid and mix to a very soft consistency.

Grease 12 patty tins and spoon some of the mixture into each tin.

Bake in a hot oven for about 25 minutes or until well browned.

Allow the buns to cool in the patty tins.

The buns are best eaten on the day they are baked.

Oven: 425°F/220°C Gas Mark 7

BROWN WHOLEMEAL BREAD

12 oz (350 g) wholemeal flour
12 oz (350 g) plain flour
1 teaspoon salt
2 teaspoons bicarbonate of soda
1 cup yeast germ (optional)
2 tablespoons bran
1 pint (600 ml/ 2½ cups) buttermilk

Combine all the dry ingredients in a large mixing bowl.

Mix in the buttermilk.

Grease an 8 inch (20 cm) round cake tin, put in the mixture and cover the top with foil.

Bake in a hot oven for 1 hour.

Oven: 425°F/220°C Gas Mark 7

SODA BREAD

Soda bread is the traditional bread of Ireland. It is round in shape and made from buttermilk or soured milk. Before the conventional oven became commonplace, bread would be baked in a fireplace hearth oven or in a griddle or heavy frying pan. Griddle made bread would be cut into sections, known as farls, before cooking.

1 lb (450 g) flour
1 teaspoon bicarbonate of soda
1 tablespoon salt
1 tablespoon ginger
½ pint (300 ml/ 1¼ cups) buttermilk or soured milk

Sieve the dry ingredients together in a large mixing bowl.

Make a well in the centre and add about half of the buttermilk.

Using a knife mix in the flour from each side.

Add enough of the remaining buttermilk to make a soft dough continuing to work the flour in from the sides.

Turn the dough onto a floured board and knead lightly for a few minutes.

Shape the dough into a round and place on a greased baking sheet or alternatively an 8 inch (20 cm) round cake tin.

Cut a deep cross into the dough to allow the bread to rise without splitting its crust.

Bake in a hot oven for about 35 minutes or until browned and risen.

Remove from the oven. If the bread is thoroughly cooked it will sound hollow when tapped on the bottom.

Oven: 425°F/220°C Gas Mark 7

WICKLOW PANCAKE

This traditional pancake is very much like an omelette and makes a substantial tea or supper dish.

2 eggs
½ pint (300 ml/ 1¼ cups) milk
2 oz (50 g) breadcrumbs
2 or 3 scallions (spring onions), chopped
Some freshly chopped herbs, i.e. a sprig of parsley, thyme or chives
2 oz (50 g) butter
Salt and pepper
Parsley for decoration

Beat the eggs with the milk.

Add the breadcrumbs, scallions, herbs and seasoning, mixing well.

Melt half the butter in a heavy based frying pan.

When the butter is frothy pour in the mixture and cook over a low heat until the top begins to set.

Turn and cook the other side, until the omelette is browned all over.

As it is fairly thick it will take a little longer cooking time than an ordinary omelette.

Dot the remaining butter on top.

Decorate with a sprig of parsley and serve.

BUTTERMILK PANCAKES

Makes about 12

It is an old custom to eat pancakes on Shrove Tuesday. Buttermilk pancakes were however served regularly at teatimes. Fresh milk may be used instead of buttermilk and the pancakes can be served with butter, jam, honey, syrup or lemon.

½ lb (225 g) flour
½ teaspoon baking powder
½ teaspoon salt
1 oz (25 g) butter
1 egg, beaten
½-¾ pint (300 ml/ 1¼ cups - 450 ml/ 2 cups)
buttermilk
Butter for frying
1 oz (25 g) caster sugar
Juice of a lemon

Sift the flour with the baking powder, salt and sugar.

Rub in the butter.

Add the beaten egg and sufficient milk to make a smooth batter.

Melt the butter in a heavy based frying pan until it begins to froth.

Pour in enough of the batter to cover the bottom of the pan.

Cook until the underneath of the pancake begins to brown.

Turn and cook the other side until brown.

Continue to cook the remaining pancakes in the frying pan, adding more butter if required.

Keep the cooked pancakes hot.

Serve sprinkled with sugar and a squeeze of lemon juice.

computarise

BOXTY PANCAKE

Boxty was popular in the north of Ireland and was traditionally eaten on Halloween. Boxty is made into bread, pancakes or dumplings. These Boxty pancakes would be served at breakfast or teatime.

½ lb (225 g) raw potatoes, peeled
½ lb (225 g) cooked mashed potatoes
½ lb (225 g) flour
1 teaspoon baking powder
1 tablespoon salt
Milk
Butter for frying

Grate the raw potatoes into a clean dry cloth.

Squeeze out the liquid through the cloth into a basin.

Reserve the liquid.

Mix together the grated potato and the mashed potato.

When clear water has risen to the top of the reserved liquid drain the liquid and mix the remaining starch with the potatoes.

Add the flour, salt and baking powder.

Add enough milk to make a smooth batter of a dropping consistency.

Melt the butter until it froths in a heavy based frying pan.

Pour in some batter and cook until brown on each side.

Continue cooking the pancakes in this way adding more butter if required, until the batter is used up.

Serve hot with butter, sugar, honey or syrup.

BOXTY BREAD

Equal amounts of:
Cooked potatoes
Raw potatoes
Flour
Salt
Fat for frying
Butter or bacon for serving

Mash the freshly cooked potatoes.

Peel and grate the raw potatoes.

Mix the raw and cooked potatoes together, and season to taste with a pinch of salt.

Work in enough flour to give a pliable dough.

Knead well and roll out.

Cut into rounds with a scone cutter.

Bake on a hot griddle.

Butter and serve hot, or alternatively fry in a frying pan and serve with bacon.

Rare Potatoes.

HOT CROSS BUNS

Makes 12 buns

Hot cross buns are traditionally eaten on Good Friday.

1 oz (25 g) yeast or 1½ teaspoons dried yeast
1 teaspoon caster sugar
1 lb (450 g) flour
1 teaspoon salt
1 teaspoon mixed spice
½ teaspoon cinnamon
½ teaspoon nutmeg
4 oz (100 g) butter or margarine
2 oz (50 g) sugar
2 oz (50 g) currants
2 oz (50 g) raisins
1 oz (25 g) candied peel
1 egg, beaten
½ pint (300 ml/ 1¼ cups) milk, warmed

For the glaze:
2 oz (50 g) sugar
3 fl oz (4½ tablespoons) milk

Cream the yeast with a teaspoon sugar.

Mix the flour, salt and spices together in a large mixing basin.

Rub in the fat.

Add the sugar, fruit and candied peel.

Make a well in the centre and pour in the beaten egg, warmed milk and yeast.

Cover the basin and leave for 20 minutes to rise.

Beat the ingredients together and work to a soft dough.

Knead the dough on a floured board for 5-10 minutes.

Cover the dough and leave in a warm place for about an hour until the dough has doubled in size.

Divide into 12 pieces and shape into rounds.

Place the rounds, well spaced, on a greased baking sheet.

Cut crosses into each bun.

Cover and leave to rise in a warm place for a further 30 minutes.

Bake in a moderately hot oven for about 20 minutes or until golden brown and put on a wire rack to cool.

For the glaze:

Dissolve the sugar with the warmed milk.

Brush the top of each bun with glaze whilst still warm.

Serve the buns immediately, buttered and with jam or honey if liked.

Oven: 400°F/200°C Gas Mark 6

TEA SCONES

Makes about 18 Scones

Hot buttered scones served with a strong cup of 'tay' at teatime have long been a favourite. Wholemeal or plain scones made with buttermilk were popular.

12 oz (350 g) wholemeal flour
4 oz (100 g) flour
2 teaspoon baking powder
A pinch of salt
1 tablespoon sugar
4 oz (100 g) butter
1 egg, beaten
Milk for mixing and glazing

Mix the flour, salt and baking powder together in a bowl.

Add the sugar.

Rub in the fat until the mixture resembles fine breadcrumbs.

Add the beaten egg and enough milk to make a soft dough.

Knead lightly and turn onto a floured surface.

Cut into rounds and place on a greased baking sheet.

Brush the top of each scone with a little milk to glaze.

Bake in a hot oven for about 15 minutes or until browned.

Oven: 420°F/220°C Gas Mark 7

Tea kettle

STIRABOUT OR PORRIDGE

Serves 2

Cereals have been grown since Neolithic times and pulses since the Iron Age. Porridge is popular for breakfast and Irish stirabout porridge made with oatmeal is famed throughout the world. In the 4th century St. Jerome wanted to abuse his enemy, Celestine, and according to the legend called him "a great fool of a man swelled out with Irish Stirabout".

Traditionally porridge was served seasoned with salt and unsweetened.

1 pint (600 ml/ 2½ cups) milk, milk and water, or water
2 oz (50 g) oatmeal
Milk or cream to serve
Sugar and honey to taste

Put the milk into a saucepan or double boiler.

Bring to the boil and sprinkle in the oatmeal with one hand whilst stirring with the other keeping the water bubbling.

Boil gently, for about 30 minutes, stirring occasionally.

Add salt to taste, continue cooking, stirring, for a few more minutes.

Serve with milk or cream, and sweetened with sugar or honey if liked.

PICKLED RED CABBAGE

Pickled Red Cabbage is traditionally served with Irish Stew and at Christmastime with Spiced Irish Beef.

For the pickled cabbage:
1 red cabbage weighing about 2 lbs (900 g) when
shredded
About 2 oz (50 g) cooking salt
2 pints (1.15 litres/ 4 cups) spiced vinegar

For the spiced* vinegar:
2 pints (1.15 litres/ 4 cups) vinegar
1 oz (25 g) blade mace
½ oz (15 g) whole allspice
½ oz (15 g) ground ginger
1 tablespoon cloves
1 cinnamon stick
6 peppercorns

* If preferred 2 oz (50 g) of pickling spice may be used instead of individual spices

To make the spiced vinegar:

Put the vinegar and spices into a saucepan.

Bring to the boil and pour into a bowl.

Allow to cool, cover the bowl and leave for at least 2 hours or up to 24 hours if a stronger flavour is liked. For the strongest flavour of all, leave the spices in cold vinegar for 1 month.

Strain the vinegar and use as required.

To make the pickled red cabbage:

Remove the tough outside leaves from the cabbage.

Shred the rest finely.

Put the cabbage in layers in a bowl, sprinkling each layer with salt.

Cover and leave for 24 hours.

Drain.

Pack the cabbage loosely into jars to finish one inch (2.5 cm) from the top.

Cover with cold spiced vinegar leaving half an inch (1 cm) space at the top.

Cover with a metal lid with a vinegar proof lining, greaseproof paper or cloth dipped in melted paraffin wax or candle grease.

Secure tightly to prevent evaporation.

Store in a cool, dry dark place.

Keep for 2 or 3 weeks before using for the flavour to develop.

Unlike other pickles, cabbage is best not stored for too long, otherwise it will lose its delicious crispness.

MINCEMEAT
Makes about 7 lbs (3.25 kg)

Meat mixed with fruit and spices was preserved for the winter by this method in early times, thus giving the preserve its name. Most modern recipes do not include meat but only beef suet. Mincemeat is traditionally used at Christmas time, especially to make Mince Pies which are very popular in Ireland.

If using at Christmas time, make the preserve in the middle of November to allow the flavour to mature. For good keeping qualities use a hard apple, such as a Wellington. Bramleys are inclined to be too juicy.

1 lb (450 g) currants
1 lb (450 g) sultanas
8 oz (225 g) stoned or seedless raisins
4 oz (100 g) glacé cherries
8 oz (225 g) mixed candied peel
4 oz (100 g) sweet almonds, blanched
1 lb (450 g) cooking apples
1 lb (450 g) soft dark brown sugar
12 oz (350 g) shredded beef suet
1 teaspoon mixed spice
1 teaspoon nutmeg
1 teaspoon cinnamon
Grated rind and juice of 2 lemons
¼ pint (150 ml/ ⅔ cup) Irish whiskey - brandy or sherry can be substituted for the whiskey

Chop or coarsely mince the currants, sultanas, raisins, glacé cherries, mixed candied peel and almonds.

Put the ingredients into a basin and mix together well.

Peel, core and chop the apples.

Mix the apples into the mixture together with the sugar, suet, spices, grated rind, juice of the lemons and the whiskey.

Stir well, cover and leave for at least 1 day or overnight. If covenient the mincemeat may be left for 2 days before potting. This improves the flavour even more.

Stir thoroughly before putting into clean, dry jars.

Tie down securely, as for jam, and store in a dark cool place.

POTTED BEEF

Makes about ½ lb (225 g)

As well as smoking and salting, potting used to be a good method of preserving fish, poultry and meat for the winter months.

Potted foods were used in the home, for packed lunches for farm workers, and on long road and sea voyages. This recipe makes a tasty paste for sandwiches or it can be served with salad. Potted Beef can be kept in a refrigerator for a few days.

1 lb (450 g) lean stewing beef
¼ pint (150 ml/ ⅔ cup) brown stock
A blade of mace
1 clove
A pinch of nutmeg
Salt and pepper
3 oz (75 g) butter
A bay leaf

Trim any fat and gristle from the meat, and cut into pieces.

Put it in an ovenproof dish with the stock, mace, clove, nutmeg and seasoning.

Cover and cook in a moderate oven for 2-3 hours.

Drain off and reserve the stock removing the mace and clove.

Mince the meat twice.

Add the stock.

Melt 1½ oz (40 g) of the butter, and stir into the mixture.

Press into one individual dish or several small ramekins.

Melt the rest of butter and pour it on top of the potted meat.

BLACKBERRY JELLY

4 lbs (1.75 kg) blackberries
Juice of 2 lemons
1 pint (600 ml/ 2½ cups) water
Sugar

Wash the blackberries and pick them over.

Put them in a preserving pan with the lemon juice and water.

Simmer the fruit gently until it is very soft.

Mash the fruit and strain through a jelly bag.

Return the strained pulp to the pan with 1 lb (450 g) of sugar to each pint (600 ml/ 2½ cups) of liquid.

Bring to the boil, stirring until the sugar has dissolved.

Boil rapidly until the mixture thickens.

Test for setting point by putting a spoonful of the jelly on a cold saucer.

Pot the jam jars and cover in the usual way.

RHUBARB AND FIG JAM

4 lbs (175 kg) rhubarb
1 lb (450 g) figs
4 oz (100 g) candied peel
4 lbs (1.75 kg) sugar

Chop the rhubarb and figs finely.

Put into a large saucepan together with the candied peel.

Cover with the sugar and leave overnight.

Bring to the boil, and boil rapidly for twenty minutes.

Cool and put into jars. Seal with purchased jam covers.

WHOLE STRAWBERRY JAM

Makes about 4 lbs (1.75 kg)

Strawberries are a popular crop and are sold from roadside stalls, particularly south of Dublin. In some areas strawberry festivals are held. To make this luxurious jam, strawberries must not be green or past their best.

4 lbs (175 kg) strawberries
4 lbs (1.75 kg) preserving sugar

Hull and wash the strawberries. Pat them dry.

Put the sugar into a preserving pan.

Heat, stirring until dissolved.

Bring to the boil and continue boiling until the syrup sets when a little is put on a cold saucer.

Carefully add the strawberries to the syrup.

Boil rapidly for 10-15 minutes.

To prevent the strawberries breaking up, avoid stirring the jam unnecessarily.

Skim off the scum from the top of the jam.

Allow to cool a little.

Stir gently to avoid the fruit rising to the top.

Pour the jam into clean, warm jars.

Whilst still hot, cover the jam with waxed disks.

Cover the jars with damp cellophane secured with a rubber band.

Label when cold with the name of the jam and date of making.

PARSLEY SAUCE

Makes ½ pint (300 ml/ 1¼ cups)

This is the traditional accompaniment to Corned Beef and Cabbage although it is also excellent with fish. The brilliant green of the parsley makes it particularly suitable for the 'Emerald Isle'.

1 oz (25 g) butter
1 oz (25 g) flour
½ pint (300 ml/ 1¼ cups) milk
Salt and pepper to taste
1 tablespoon chopped parsley

Melt the butter in a saucepan.

Stir in the flour to make a roux, and cook for a few moments, stirring continuously.

Gradually stir in the milk.

Bring to the boil, season to taste and simmer until the sauce thickens, stirring occasionally.

Stir in the chopped parsley.

CELERY SAUCE

This sauce is used as an accompaniment to roast and boiled turkey, but is also excellent with mutton or rabbit.

1 head of celery
2 oz (50 g) turkey stock
2 oz (50 g) butter
2 oz (50 g) flour
¼ pint (150 ml/ ⅔ cup) milk
Salt and pepper
¼ pint (150 ml/ ⅔ cup) cream

Wash the celery, and chop it using the heart and the green tops.

Put in a saucepan with the turkey stock.

Bring to the boil, and simmer for about 15 minutes or until tender.

Drain and retain the liquid.

Rub the celery through a sieve or blend in a liquidiser.

Melt the butter in a saucepan.

Stir in the flour to make a roux.

Cook for a few moments, still stirring.

Gradually add the stock, stirring continually until the sauce thickens.

Stir in the milk and the celery purée.

Season to taste.

Add the cream, but do not allow the sauce to boil again.

Serve hot in a sauce boat.

ONION SAUCE

Makes about 12 fl oz (350 ml/1½ cups)

Serve with lamb, pork chops or fried liver. If piled on toast and topped
with hard-boiled eggs it will make a delicious light supper or lunch.

2 onions
1 oz (25 g) butter
1 oz (25 g) flour
8 fl oz (250 ml/ 1 cup) cream
Salt and pepper

Peel and slice the onions.

Put in a saucepan of cold water.

Bring to the boil and simmer until tender.

Drain and rub through a sieve.

Melt the butter, and stir in the flour to make a roux.

Cook, stirring, for a few moments.

Gradually add the milk, still stirring.

Bring to the boil, season to taste and simmer until the sauce
thickens, stirring occasionally.

Add the puréed onions, and stir in the cream.

Reheat but do not allow the sauce to boil again.

APPLE SAUCE

This sauce is excellent with goose, duck and pork. It should be fairly tart to serve with these dishes. If the apples are too sweet, a little lemon juice may be added. If the sauce is required a little sweeter, add some sugar.

1 lb (450 g) apples
1 oz (25 g) butter
A pinch of nutmeg (optional)

Peel, core and slice the apples, using a stainless steel knife to avoid discolouration.

Put into a saucepan with the nutmeg.

Cook gently over a low heat until the apples are pulped.

Beat with a wooden spoon until smooth or put through a sieve or liquidizer.

Heat the sauce again, and add the butter.

Serve hot in a sauceboat.

LEMON SAUCE

Excellent with ham or bacon.

1 oz (25 g) butter
1 oz (25 g) flour
½ pint (300 ml/ 1¼ cups) ham stock
The juice and grated peel of a lemon

Melt the butter in a saucepan.

Stir in the flour and cook to make a roux.

Heat the stock and pour it slowly onto the roux, stirring continuously.

Bring to the boil still stirring.

Mix the juice and grated lemon peel into the sauce.

Serve hot.

SAVOURY ANTRIM SAUCE

1 onion
2 oz (50 g) flour
1 tablespoon tomato purée
15 fl oz (450 ml/2 cups) stock
2 oz (50 g) butter
8 fl oz (250 ml/ 1 cup) red wine
1 tablespoon dry mustard
Salt and pepper to taste
1 teaspoon sugar

Peel and chop the onion finely.

Melt the butter and fry the onions until soft.

Stir in the flour to make a roux.

Pour on the stock stirring all the time.

Bring to the boil and simmer for about 15 minutes.

Stir in the mustard, tomato purée, wine, sugar and seasoning.

Cook for a further 10 minutes.

IRISH MIST PUDDING SAUCE

Irish Mist is a liqueur made from whiskey, honey and herbs. It can be used for cooking, baking or as a sauce for puddings. It also makes a very good liqueur coffee.

¼ pint (150 ml/ ⅔ cup) milk, warmed
2 oz (50 g) sugar
2 egg yolks
½ glass Irish Mist liqueur

Whisk together the sugar, warmed milk and egg yolks until frothy.

Add the Irish Mist liqueur and continue whisking as the sauce thickens.

Serve immediately with steamed puddings such as plum pudding.

SWEET WHISKEY SAUCE

This is a basic white sauce flavoured with whiskey to serve with puddings.

2 oz (50 g) butter or margarine
1 oz (25 g) flour
1 pint (600 ml/ 2½ cups) milk
2 oz (50 g) sugar
2 tablespoons of Irish whiskey

Melt the fat in a saucepan.

Stir in the flour, and cook gently still stirring to make a roux.

Gradually stir in the milk and the sugar.

Bring to the boil, still stirring and cook for about five minutes until the sauce has thickened.

Stir in the whiskey and serve.

HOME-MADE CUSTARD SAUCE

Makes 1 pint (600 ml/ 2½ cups)

This sauce has been made for centuries to accompany sweet puddings. Using the simple dairy products that are readily available in the country, it has always been popular in Ireland. It is well worth making home-made custard. It is quick and easy to do, and tastes delicious, especially if some cream is added to the milk.

¾ pint (450 ml/ 2 cups) milk
¼ pint (150 ml/ ⅔ cup) cream
2 eggs
1 teaspoon vanilla flavouring
1 oz (25 g) sugar or to taste

Put a saucepan of cold water on the stove to boil.

Beat the eggs, sugar and vanilla flavouring together.

Heat the milk and stir it into the egg mixture.

Put the custard into a bowl and stand it in the water to heat over a moderate heat.

Stir until all the sugar is dissolved and the mixture thickens.

Do not allow the custard to boil, or it will curdle.

Put into a serving jug.

Serve hot or cold.

If using cold, cover the jug to prevent a skin forming.

BUTTERMILK

Buttermilk is a good refreshing health giving drink. Every Irish farmhouse would have a churnful of buttermilk left over after butter making and there would also be a jug of buttermilk on the table for drinking. It is still commonly used in the baking of many bread, scone and cake recipes. Here is a method of making buttermilk at home.

½ oz (15 g) sugar
½ oz (15 g) yeast
½ pint (300 ml/ 1¼ cups) warmed water
½ pint (300 ml/ 1¼ cups) milk

Cream the sugar with the yeast.

Mix the milk with the warmed water.

Gradually stir the sugar into the yeast.

Cover and leave at room temperature for at least a day.

The liquid should smell slightly sour and taste like buttermilk.

Strain and the buttermilk is ready to use.

SLOE GIN

Sloes should be gathered after the first frost. They are the fruit of the blackthorn which grows well in Ireland. This drink can also be made with damsons.

1¾ pints (1 litre) bottle of gin
12 oz (350 g) sloes
10 oz (275 g) sugar
1 oz (25 g) chopped almonds or almond essence to taste

Wash and prick the sloes with a fork.

Put into bottle with the sugar and almonds.

Fill with gin. Cork and seal.

Leave in a cool place for at least 3 months.

Shake daily for 14 days and then once a week.

Strain, rebottle and cork.

CARRAGHEEN DRINK

Carragheen is a good drink for bedtime as it is believed to help sleeplessness.

½ oz (15 g) Carragheen Moss
2 pints (1.15 litres/ 4 cups) of milk or water
A little lemon rind
Sugar to sweeten to taste

Wash the moss thoroughly.

Put into a saucepan with the milk or water and the lemon rind. Bring to the boil very slowly.

Continue boiling for about 5 minutes.

Strain and sweeten to taste.

WHISKEY PUNCH

Whiskey punch has been popular in Ireland for centuries. It is traditionally drunk at Christmas although it makes a good bedtime drink.

7 fl oz (200 ml/¾ cup) water
1 measure Irish whiskey
2 teaspoons sugar
3 cloves
2 slices of lemon

Put the sugar into a pan with the water.

Bring to the boil and stir until the sugar is dissolved.

Remove from the heat.

Add the whiskey, cloves and lemon slices.

Pour into a warmed ½ pint (300 ml/ 1¼ cups) tumbler and serve.

IRISH COFFEE

Serves 1

Irish coffee was invented in 1938 by the Chef at Shannon Airport. He would serve Irish coffee to cold travellers who had been journeying along the Shannon, the largest river in Ireland, in the old style flying boats. It is now renowned and enjoyed all over the world.

A jigger of Irish whiskey
Strong black coffee
2 heaped teaspoons sugar or to taste
2 tablespoons double cream or whipped cream

Warm a stemmed whiskey glass.

Pour in the Irish whiskey and fill to three quarters full with strong coffee.

Stir in the sugar until dissolved.

Top up with the pure cream poured gently over a teaspoon or add lightly whipped cream on top.

The drink should not be stirred after the cream has been added.

BLACK VELVET

Serves 1

This is a very good drink which goes well with oysters. It is made with stout and champagne but could be made with a sparkling wine for parties.

¼ pint (150 ml/ ⅔ cup) Guinness or stout
¼ pint (150 ml/ ⅔ cup) champagne, chilled

Mix the stout and champagne.

Pour into a long glass and serve.

DATE AND COCONUT FUDGE

1 lb (450 g) soft brown sugar
2 oz (50 g) butter
1 tablespoon desiccated coconut
8 fl oz (¼ litre/ 1 cup) milk
2 tablespoons cream
2 oz (50 g) dates, chopped

Put the sugar, butter, desiccated coconut, milk and cream into a heavy based saucepan.

Heat gently until the sugar dissolves and the butter melts.

Boil for about 15 minutes.

Test the mixture by putting a drop into cold water to form a soft ball.

Take the pan from the heat.

Add the chopped dates and beat the mixture until it is thick.

Pour the mixture into a greased tin and leave to set.

Just before it sets mark the fudge into squares with a sharp knife and break into pieces when cold.

YELLOWMAN

> 'Did you treat your Mary Ann to dulse and Yellowman
> At the Ould Lammas Fair at Bally Castle'.

A traditonal and popular sweet in Ireland, yellowman is still sold at country fairs. It was usually brought in a lump to fairs, and broken off as required. Famous yellowman maker, Dick Murray of Lurgan, would sometimes put a halfpenny in the sweet before it set. There was much competition and excitement to find the lucky piece.

1 oz (25 g) butter
8 oz (225 g) brown sugar
1 lb (450 g) golden syrup
2 tablespoons water
1 tablespoon baking soda

Melt the butter in a saucepan, tilting the pan so that it is well greased.

Add the sugar, syrup and water, stirring until the sugar is dissolved.

Boil until it is brittle when a little is dropped into cold water.

Stir in the soda.

Turn onto a greased surface.

Fold the edges into the centre, and pull when sufficiently cool.

Pull until pale in colour.

THE BEST COLD CREAM

'The best cold cream that is really softening and healing to the skin.

Take two ounces of white soap, half an ounce of spearmint and a pint of sweet oil, put all together in a jar place on the hob close to a good fire, let the ingredients melt and remain molten for some time, stirring them occasionally, when cold, the preparation is complete, scent of any kind is injurious to the skin. '

Acknowledgements

Grateful thanks are extended to the many people of Ireland who have contributed towards this collection of recipes, especially:

Margaret Browne of Ballymakeigh House, Killeagh, Co. Cork for Cream of Mushroom Soup, Potatoes in Chive Cream and Cheese Scones.

Joe Murray, Chef of White's Hotel, Wexford, Co. Wexford for Sole and Mussels Captain's Style and Wexford Mussels in Rum Sauce.

Pat Kell, Executive Head Chef of the Dunadry Inn, Dunadry, Co. Antrim for Lough Neagh Bouillabaisse.

Gerard Hanratty, Director of the Howth Lodge Hotel, Howth, Co. Dublin for Gaelic Chicken.

Re Kinsella of Bray, Co. Wicklow for Brown Wholemeal Bread and Orange Mousse.

Peggy Batty of Sevenoaks, Kent and Clonakilty, Co. Cork for Savoury Mince, Pork and Apple Stew, Apple Pie, Rock Cakes and Bread and Butter Pudding.

Father Thomas Quinn of Sevenoaks, Kent and Rathdowney, Co. Leix for Dublin Coddle.

Jean McKean of the Hall Greene Farm Guest House, Lifford, Co. Donegal for Champ or Poundies, Hall Green Cookies, Carragheen Drink, Apple Soufflé Cheesecake, Oatmeal Cakes, Irish Potato Bread or Fadge and Boxty Bread.

K. Morton of Bushmills, Co. Antrim for information.

Sarah McNamara of Parteen, Co. Limerick for Halloween Brack, Limerick Side Salad, Gaelic Steak with Irish Whiskey Sauce, Parteen Pudding, Crubeens and Guinness and Wexford Brownies.

Ita Cross of Bangor, Co. Down for Mammy's Brown Buns and Rhubarb and Fig Jam.

Michael Cole of Tralee, Co. Kerry for Colcannon, Ling with Onion Sauce and information.

Bonnie Hughes-Quinn of Graiguenamanagh, Co. Kilkenny for information and Mutton Pies.

Forman's of Howth, Co. Dublin for information on methods of traditional fish smoking.

The King Sitric Restaurant and Forman's of Howth, Co. Dublin for Whiting Baked with Onions, Haddock with Cream.

The National Library of Ireland, Kildare Street, Dublin for information; and for Best Cold Cream from the Downpatrick collection of handwritten recipes dated 1815-1846.

THE COUNTRY RECIPE SERIES

Available now @ £1.95 each

Cambridgeshire	Lancashire
Cornwall	Leicestershire
Cumberland & Westmorland	Norfolk
Derbyshire	Northumberland & Durham
Devon	Oxfordshire
Dorset	Somerset
Essex	Suffolk
Gloucestershire	Sussex
Hampshire	Warwickshire
Herefordshire & Worcestershire	Wiltshire
Kent	Yorkshire

Available @ £2.95 each:

Scottish Country Recipes
Welsh Country Recipes
English Country Recipes
Irish Country Recipes

All these books are available at your local bookshop or newsagent, or can be ordered direct from the publisher. Just tick the titles you require and fill in the form below. Prices and availability subject to change without notice.

Ravette Books Limited, 3 Glenside Estate, Star Road, Partridge Green, Horsham, West Sussex RH13 8RA.

Please send a cheque or postal order, and allow the following for postage and packing. UK 25p for one book and 10p for each additional book ordered.

Name ....

Address..

....

....